CHOSEN

God's relentless pursuit of His wandering child

The Ron Rockey story

Pacific Press® Publishing Association
Nampa, Idaho
Oshawa, Ontario, Canada
www.pacificpress.com

Edited by Bonnie Tyson-Flyn
Designed by Dennis Ferree
Cover photo by Orion Press / Black Sheep

The accuracy of all quotations and references is the responsibility of the author.

All Scripture quotations are taken from the New International Bible.

Additional copies of this book may be purchased at
http://www.adventistbookcenter.com

Library of Congress Cataloging-in-Publication Data:

ISBN 0-8163-1900-6

01 02 03 04 05 • 5 4 3 2 1

CONTENTS

DEDICATION

To all of the men who have played a father role in my life until I could come to know the heavenly Father. Thank you!

Stanley Rockey, who did the best he could with what he had. I understand you now.

Grandpa Miller, who patiently taught me how to tie my shoes and plant a garden.

John Rebstock, who put up with my rebelliousness, my drunkenness, and my foul mouth, and who put it all "in the past" to maintain a loving relationship with me to this day.

Charles E. Ward, whether human or angelic, who secured my release from the brig, mentored me lovingly, and guided me to the church I have embraced.

Leonard Haswell, who looked enough like my birth father to be a twin brother, and who took this "boy" under his paternal wing, taught and loved me while in Tennessee's "big house," introduced me to Jesus, and applauded at each baby step I took along my way.

Pastor Joseph Damazo, who took me into his heart and his home, who taught me how to love "the saints," picked me up when discouraged, introduced me to Nancy, then married us and dedicated our daughters. You are loved!

James Hallas, Nancy's father, who truly became the father mine couldn't be. He could not have loved me more if I were his very own. He supported me in every way possible and encouraged me through the tough undergraduate years. Finally when I was in ministry, he was there to play the piano for every important event, to give me sound advice, and to be the best possible grandfather to our daughters! I miss you, Dad!

Ralph Larson, who was my college professor. He saw some good in me, brought it out, and has been a source of comfort and encouragement since.

Stu Jayne, who was my first conference president in ministry. He trained me with an iron fist in a velvet glove, and I did some resisting! Yet I am grateful for his guidance, his love, and the encouragement he gave along the way.

Harry Anderson, who was my first elder in my first pastorate. Without Harry, I know that I would no longer be in ministry. Harry was at my side to support, to paint ceilings, embellish a painting, or give me an original. His arms were always open to console.

and

to the many others sent across my path to advise, to support, and to encourage.

You were a gift from a loving heavenly Daddy
who wanted "His boy" to succeed. I am grateful!

ACKNOWLEDGEMENTS

John and Phyllis Rebstock, Ron's sister/mother and brother-in-law, who filled in the blank spots of Ron's childhood circumstances and experiences.

Priscilla S. Perry, our friend who read and re-read, editing as she encouraged the completion of this book.

Douglas and Deb Haefner, who let us come to their home to hide and fed us as well, while we finished the manuscript.

Velma Ellstrom, who was in charge of the Faith For Today Bible Correspondence School while Ron was a prisoner at Nashville State Penitentiary. Somehow Ron's name was intriguing to her, and she insisted on keeping up the correspondence with him until he completed his course. She then accompanied her minister-husband to the mission field, where they served for a number of years.

Thirty-five years passed, and we were conducting a funeral in Phoenix, Arizona. Velma was in attendance. Following the service, Velma approached us and asked if Ron Rockey was really Ron's name. "Did you ever live in Nashville, Tennessee? Did you live at the 'Big House' there?" she asked. As Ron answered each of her questions, tears began to pour down Velma's cheeks.

"I have been praying for you for thirty-five years," she said. "I was one of the women who graded your Bible correspondence lessons while you were in prison, and I have never forgotten your name. It was musical to me, and since that time, I have prayed for you every day. I had no idea what had become of you until this very day."

Velma was publicly honored for her faithfulness at the Loma Linda celebration of Faith For Today's fiftieth anniversary.

All along the way, God had supplied surrogate fathers until Ron could understand the love of his heavenly Father, but until recently, we had no idea that he also had supplied a praying "mother in Israel" to intercede in his behalf.

INTRODUCTION

Have you ever pressed your nose against the window of a pet shop and watched the puppies play in the wood chips? Something about those innocent little cuties steals the hearts of most kids—and don't we all have a bit of child in us?

Just the other day, we went with our friends to look at some pups. You see, Minnie, our loved miniature schnauzer disappeared about three and a half years ago during a rare Phoenix rainstorm. We made more effort to find her than some people would make over a lost child, but she was gone. We looked for her, called her name, took a second look at every schnauzer we encountered just to be sure it wasn't "our girl." But our effort has been in vain. Minnie has not been found, except perhaps by someone who wanted her very much and is holding on tight, lest she be seen by the original "Mom and Dad."

As we stood in the barn where these puppies were raised, it was hard to know where to look first. The place was full of many pens, with litters of one of nine dog breeds in each pen. There were even two litters of "snorkies," a combination of schnauzers and Yorkshire terriers, and, yes, we had a look at those also. But after such a wonder dog as Minnie, nothing but a purebred schnauzer would do!

Now when you look at puppies, especially if you know anything about what to look for in a dog, you look at several things: their bite (how their upper and lower teeth come together), their hips and hind legs, the shape of their head, their ears, their coat. The list is long. And then you watch for disposition. How do they respond to people? Do they appear to be hyper? Can they hear well? Will they follow you?

Then you ask another question: Do you want this dog as a pet, for show, or for breeding? If you plan to breed the dog, you focus on the bloodline. If you plan to show the dog, you choose one within a certain weight and size. If you want this pup for a pet, you want to be attracted especially to him or her, and you want a pup that responds to you, snuggles into your neck, feels comfy in your arms.

How different it is when our heavenly Father comes to choose a child. At the moment of conception, sight unseen, He places a SOLD mark on our foreheads. "I have chosen you, you belong to Me, you are Mine!"

Unfortunately, we are like deaf, blind, poor-quality pups, but God doesn't care! He knows the family into which we came. He knows that the bloodline is defective, that our disposition is more like the devil's. And He also knows what He can do with a pup like us. He knows that He can call us, and we'll eventually hear His voice and respond. He knows that He can feed us on His Word, and eventually we will grow. He knows that He can train us, and in time we will obtain a character like His own, so that we can, like the faithful dog, love our Master and obey Him.

To God, it doesn't matter where He has to go to draw us to Him, because no place is too far, too evil, or too frightening to reach down and snatch us away from the din into the peacefulness of His arms.

This is the story of one young "pup" that God chose at conception. It is the saga of his adventures, running from a Parent he could not see, searching for both a human father and a heavenly Father he could not find. It is the story of a choosing, a calling that began in his early years and finally was answered behind the bars of Nashville Penitentiary. It is the story of a longing that could be filled only by a father, the fathers provided along the way, and finally, going home, where his Father awaited him.

P.S. Yes we chose a schnauzer puppy! She's a little girl named Medora Joy.

CHAPTER 1

I huddled under the bridge, clutching the November 1, 1958, newspaper. I was alone again, hidden, solitary. I liked being alone better than being in a crowd, better than being at the house with the strangers who were my family. The old hiding place was noisy, but at least the familiar roar of the cars and trucks overhead helped to drown out my racing thoughts: I am unwanted; I always have been. Why is it that I'm not like other people? What makes me feel so different from everybody else? I don't know!

It was the morning after Halloween, a holiday I had never cared for. The evening before Dad had dressed up in an old white sheet, with little holes cut out for eyes and a mouth. That was odd because I had never seen him play before. Then he had hidden beside a little bridge and made ghost noises to frighten the little kids as they went past. I wondered what prompted him to do that.

I finally got the courage to open the newspaper, to look for the obituary section. There it was: "**Stanley C. Rockey—dies of a heart attack.**" There was my name at the end of the article, just one of the "survived by." That's a relief! But if I am a survivor, why don't I feel alive today? I don't feel the same; it's as if part of me died too.

It was cold and damp under the bridge that crossed the Arkansas River in Little Rock, but there I could be alone. I went there often just to think my own thoughts and stay out of everyone's way. There I could could get lost in distorted fantasies, I could cry, I could be totally me—unconnected to anyone. Under the bridge I could slug down the booze I sneaked out of Dad's liquor cabinet and go to a place in my mind that was far away from the garbage of this life. Far away from the constant bickering at home. Far enough away to not feel Ma's distance—her unwillingness to talk, to touch, to even call me "son." Far enough away to not wince whenever Dad came home in a rage.

I thought about my older brother George, the constant source of aggravation and the whipping boy for Dad and Mom's annoyances. At least half the time he took a beating for their anger or tension over something that had gone wrong at work or between them. He took it for everyone—George the scapegoat. How many times I had watched as George was marched down to the furnace room to be beaten. The sound of that awful razor strop being slapped across his body gave me chills! And what's worse was Mother, sitting on the basement steps, egging Daddy on to beat George harder and longer for stuff he'd done a long time before and had already taken a beating for. Why would a mother do that? Was she trying to stay on the right side of Dad, wanting him to take out his rage on George instead of on her?

After those beatings, George would come to bed in the room we shared, and he would hug himself and rock back and forth in agony. The beatings went on until he was seventeen or so and left to go into the military.

Peachy was a couple years older than George; she left home to get married when she was fifteen. She would come into our room when he was rocking himself in bed for comfort and beat him on the head with her high-heel shoe to try to make him quit sobbing and moaning. That poor guy got it from everybody. Occasionally he did something to deserve punishment, but what he got wasn't punishment—it was torture!

I sat under the bridge wondering how parents could choose one of their kids to pick on, one to punish for everyone, while others went unpunished regardless of what they did. How could parents pick another kid to ignore? That was me—unnoticed. George was picked on, and I was avoided. Neither of my parents seemed to care where I went or when I came home.

When I was little, they would punish me by taking my precious things away. I'll never forget the Christmas I got the train; it was gone by noon. What in the world did I do that was so awful that they would take away my one present? Or was it that I was just not really included in the family? Maybe I didn't really belong to them.

Peachy got all the good stuff. Phyllis, my other sister, never got much, but at least she didn't get beatings—neither of the girls did. But they were smart enough to leave home young! And when Bobby came along when I was six or so, Mother doted over him all the time; he could do no wrong in her sight! Little Judy, though, born a year later, seemed lost like me. Considering that she was the last one of the second batch of kids and George was the last one in the first batch, I wondered if she felt as isolated as he did.

Actually my parents' friends were more important to them than we were. The Eastermans came over every Saturday night for Mother's homemade pastries, and then they played cards and drank coffee and booze until real late Saturday night. Yeah, that's probably why my parents rarely went to church; they just sent me by myself. They were probably hung over.

I read the obituary in the newspaper again to verify that it was really true, that Dad was really dead. I was terrified of leaving the hiding place under the bridge and returning to the house. They always said that I would never amount to anything, that I never could do anything right. Last night I proved them right. I couldn't save my father from dying. I called the ambulance first, and I'm sure I told them to come to 1217 Garland Avenue. Then I called the doctor. He came to the right address, so how could I have screwed up the address I told the ambulance people? They claimed they went to the wrong address.

I had gone to bed early. Sometime during the night, Mom woke me up, hysterically telling me to come to their bedroom because Dad was dying. Dad was choking—kind of gurgling, and his skin was bluish. I did everything I had learned to earn the Scout's life-saving honor, but it did no good. He just got grayer and clammy cold with no pulse. Mom just kept pacing and crying. Finally when the doctor arrived, he opened his old black bag and got out a syringe and gave Dad a shot in his chest. Still Dad didn't take a breath. When the ambulance driver was wheeling Dad out on that stretcher, he said that they had gone to the wrong address.

As I saw it, I had blown it twice: I couldn't save my dad's life and I must have given the ambulance people the wrong address. So I murdered my dad because I couldn't do anything right. I reasoned that Dad was too angry all the time to be allowed to go to heaven. But I didn't want Dad to go to hell, to burn all the time, to be tortured that much for being hot-tempered. If it was my fault he died, I decided that he should be able to go to heaven. He did have six kids, and most of us weren't so good; no wonder he was furious so often. I reasoned that a murderer really deserved hell, but someone who was always angry—and I was one reason for his anger—didn't deserve hell.

I decided to try to bargain with God for Dad's sake.

"God. If You're really there like they say You are, I want to make a bargain with You. The paper says that Dad died last night. I tried to save him, but I couldn't. So if You'll take him to heaven, I'll take his place in hell. If You will take Dad to heaven, I'll never ask You, never again in my whole life, for anything else for myself. I promise! Thanks God. Amen."

CHAPTER 2

An occasional scream punctuated the groans that came from the attic. Finally Renata was in full labor. During the previous ten months, she had attempted to deny the existence of the child growing inside her. These were ten months of terror, fearing her husband's reaction when he learned of the pregnancy. Renata and Stanley had already decided to have no more children; the existing three were a burden to feed and clothe. Eight years had passed before this pregnancy.

It was wartime, and food was scarce. The budget was already stretched to its limits. Hotdog soup for a family of three children, with only one hotdog to flavor the entire pot of soup, was all that Renata could afford. If Stanley was at home, he would get the hotdog, for which she had bartered with the butcher. The vegetables were those she had scavenged from the bin behind the local grocery store. Wrinkled carrots, shriveled celery, discolored onions and potatoes were better than nothing at all, and she would carefully wash and trim them for the soup.

Renata worked some to supplement their income at her family's bakery, but business there was so slow that it was hardly worth the effort of going in. She was, however, allowed to bring home day-old bread for free; so she showed up for a few hours' work to feel entitled to the handouts. Times were tough, but she did her best to make ends meet and to stretch the budget to meet the needs of her growing family. Fortunately, Renata was a clever seamstress. From worn-out adult clothes, she could design and sew clothes for the children. Renata could stretch a nickel into a dollar.

During the war, Stanley's poor eyesight kept him from military service overseas. Instead, he was sent to Manitowoc shipyards as a sheet-metal worker, installing heat and air conditioning on battle ships and submarines. His infrequent trips home had made it easier for Renata to hide her bulging abdomen and the truth about her pregnancy.

Renata had good reason be concerned about Stanley's reaction. He would be livid! How was she going to tell him that there was a fourth child to feed? How would she explain that she had kept the truth from him these months while he was away? Would he yell and scream as she had seen him do in times past when he was upset? Would he think that this child was not his own? What would become of their relationship?

They had a deep love, but their marriage was marred by Stanley's temper. Stanley was prone to drinking, and when he was inebriated, his temper flared easily. He was one of seven brothers, all of whom were hot-tempered. Their mother Marie was a tiny German woman who was cold and bitter. She kept her children at an emotional distance, longing for love and acceptance, but never experiencing it. Their dad was a quiet man who rarely spoke to either his wife or his seven sons, but they did see him rage on occasion. All the boys longed for closeness with a woman, but because of the patterns learned in childhood, could not seem to achieve what they needed. Stanley was no exception.

Renata, too, was of German decent. Her father was a baker—breads and pastries were part of her heritage. Her culinary abilities were part of her attractiveness to Stanley. While she was a stunningly beautiful woman when she married Stanley, she was never slim. Her beauty was so exceptional that one ignored her size. Renata was pensive yet fun-loving. She said very little about herself and found it difficult to share her thoughts and her feelings. Growing up in a hard-working family, she became a determined worker herself, who stayed up late at night to get all her chores accomplished. Before the war, she spent Saturdays in the kitchen, mixing bread and pastry dough in her huge enamel dishpan, and baking kuchen and sticky pecan rolls. She had learned well from her father Henry, who ran Miller's Bakery for most of his life.

While being deeply in love with her husband, Renata was somewhat afraid of his temper, so she tiptoed around him, determined to avoid disagreements or conflict of any kind. Rather than risking arguments, she would stuff her negative emotions deep inside, where they would eventually resurface as physical symptoms. When Stanley was at home, she forced herself to act carefree and affectionate.

Stanley and Renata's children were deeply affected by their dad's temper and their mother's betrayal of their brother George. As a result, most of the siblings were emotionally starved and were disconnected from their parents and from each other.

Even the child in Renata's womb knew that he was not wanted. Unconsciously, he had refused to send out the hormone to his mother that would instigate the birth process. Renata's fears had affected the boy even before his birth; her attempt to deny her pregnancy had set the stage for years of emotional emptiness.

The actual delivery was a blur of pain far worse than the three previous births, understandable since she had carried this child for a full ten months, and at birth he weighed ten-and-a-half pounds. But Renata's mental pain was even greater than her physical pain, and she escaped into a world of her own where she would be protected from responsibilities and could deny the existence of the fourth child.

Little was known about postpartum psychosis at that time. Everyone assumed that her body would quickly recover from shock of delivering such a large child, and she would once again take up her role of mother. At first the baby had been put to her breast, but no bond formed. She held baby Ron mechanically in her arms, but she could not hold him in her heart.

Peachy, Phyllis, and George had to fend for themselves. Their mother was not cooking or caring for them; she just sat and stared. When the new baby cried, she didn't pick him up, didn't feed him, didn't cuddle him. Baby Ron continued to scream.

Phyllis, the nine-year-old sister, finally couldn't bear the baby's crying. First she prepared a bottle and gingerly approached his crib. Scared but determined to help the screaming baby, Phyllis picked him up. The crying continued, but he seemed to gradually stop the shaking. Finally she took the courage to offer the bottle; much to Phyllis's relief, the baby immediately began to suck. Phyllis relaxed back into the rocker and held her little brother in her arms as he emptied the bottle. Her next chore was changing his diaper. Renata hadn't done that for a very long time. He also needed to be bathed and dressed in clean clothes. Nine-year-old Phyllis managed those tasks and then rocked baby Ron to sleep.

Renata continued to stare into space, ignoring her three school-age children and newborn baby.

What would these circumstances do to the little brother whom Phillis was beginning to love?

CHAPTER 3

Stanley came home for a surprise visit, and he was the one shocked! At last the truth was out. The family crib had been reassembled again after eight years of being stored in the attic. And in that well-used crib was a handsome, chubby baby boy. Stan took one look at him and recognized instantly that this dumpling was his son. To everyone's surprise, Stanley didn't fly into a rage. Giving a little chuckle, Stanley picked the baby up out of the crib. This was no featherweight child. At that moment, Ron was given the name that stuck for years, the name he came to hate. "Butch," the nickname given by his father, was related to his size.

Quickly it became apparent to Stanley that something was different about his wife.

Phyllis was caring for Ron, and Renata seemed to be in an altered state in which reality and responsibility were abandoned. She clung to her husband, but was out of touch with her children, particularly with the new baby. Stanley decided that Renata needed a break from the stress of caring for the children, so he hired a sixteen-year-old neighbor girl to care for the baby while Peachy, Phyllis, and George were in school. When the children came home from school, Phyllis was to take over the mothering, and the nanny would go home until the next morning. Stanley planned to take Renata back to Manitowoc with him, so she could recover her health away from the stressful added responsibility of a son she never wanted.

No one questioned the feasibility of a nine-year-old child adequately caring for an infant, but Stanley was not particularly concerned about

Phyllis or baby Ron. He just needed to restore the woman he had married. He reasoned that he was as responsible as she was for the pregnancy, and he would take that responsibility seriously. Stanley and Renata left the next day for the shipyard town, where he hoped that being away from an overload of demands and being with him in the evening would bring her back to emotional health.

Phyllis became Ron's nine-year-old mother, as well as the caretaker of her older sister Peachy and her younger brother George. Obviously, these were overwhelming and inappropriate tasks for a nine-year-old, but she did her best. She would care for the baby she had come to love, and her siblings would have to fend for themselves as best they could.

While little Ron grew and became an adorable physically healthy baby, there was no stability and no consistency in his life. Women seemed to come and go as often as his need for food. Sometimes his nine-year-old sister Phyllis met his physical needs; other times the sixteen-year-old nanny fed or changed him. Dad, who should have been the model and the stabilizing force, was missing. And when he did come home, Dad did not connect emotionally with the boy. Mother, the woman inside of whom he lived for ten long months, was also missing. She was not there to talk, cuddle, or sing to her newborn. The thing needed the most for emotional and physical health—safe and gentle parental touch—was totally absent for this beautiful baby boy. Even when Mother would come home and stay for a few weeks, she busied herself baking delicacies or sewing but not connecting emotionally. She was there to cook and bake as if she were storing up food for the children so that she could leave again to be with Stanley. Obviously, he was the most important part of her life, and the kids were the outward manifestation of their love and need for each other.

During the important time when the infant's brain is taking in information through all the senses and the emotions, baby Ron was left alone for long periods of time. Nine-year-old Phyllis was his safest companion and nurturer, so Ron began to build a bond with Phyllis that would always comfort him when times got tough.

Ron learned how to amuse himself in the absence of playmates or caregivers. In order to be fed, he would have to throw temper tantrums; when he was at the point of passing out from hunger, someone would prop a bottle against the crib side. Life was a round of screaming to get needs met. But the screaming did not make him popular with his brother and sisters, so all too often he was ignored, isolated, and avoided, even when he wasn't screaming. One message was clear, even before he had language: nobody wanted Ron.

Ron's care did not improve much when Renata recovered from the severe depression that had plagued her. She had not been warm and cuddly with her first three children and was even colder to Ron. To her, Ron was still a complication, and she really did not know how to relate with him. Even though the three older siblings were at school during the day and the baby was home alone with Mother, she didn't have time for him.

Renata did indeed have the burden of caring for a house and four kids. There was always cooking, sewing, laundry, and cleaning to do. Her bigger burden, however, was meeting Stanley's demands in order to earn his continued acceptance and love. She was obsessive about preparing for Stanley to come home, for he was a fussy man who demanded perfectly laundered clothes and slacks ironed with a razor-sharp crease. He expected an abundant meal every evening, even if the budget was strained. To Stanley, sitting down to a large dinner was a sign that his wife was caring for him adequately and doing her share of the work for the family.

To entertain himself, Ron spent long hours playing by himself with the few toys he had. Since the family lived in a little house near the railroad, waiting for and watching the train was his favorite pastime. Sometimes Ron would run out to the little picket fence in front of the house to listen for the whistle, and on cold or rainy days, he would press his little nose against the windowpane to wait for his best friend, the train.

After the war was over, Stanley was usually home for the evening meal. Peachy, Phyllis, George, Ron, and Renata all sat in their designated seats, and Stanley would sit at the head of the table. Suppertime became an unpleasant ritual of criticizing the children's school performance or George's behavior. Stanley would make his right hand into a fist and pound on the table with such force that the dishes would dance. The children were afraid of him, and suppertime was an unpleasant, frightening time, to say the least!

Renata had a rule that the children couldn't reach beyond their plates for something they wanted. The children were supposed to ask for someone to pass it. Frequently they had Renata's fork jabbed into the backs of their hands because they reached for something.

Ron's memory of one holiday meal gives a window into the way he was generally treated: "I can't recall if it was a Thanksgiving or Christmas dinner we were having, but I do remember that we were having turkey. I wanted a drumstick! There was always a contest of who could get one of them first, and on this one occasion, I won out. Probably I had made a real fuss about it, because my mother and dad seemed aggravated that I got it. Now the rule was that you had to eat everything on your plate, but on the table there was also dressing, mashed potatoes, and several vegetables, and I had a little of everything on my plate. Well, of course I couldn't eat the entire drumstick, which enraged my mother. I can't remember which parent, but one of them plunked me on a dining room chair away from the table and told me I had to sit there forever. I was used to entertaining myself, used to being alone, so it was no big deal to me. I have no clue what I was doing to keep myself occupied, but whatever it was, that also incensed my parents. They were furious that I wasn't crying and begging to be let off the chair. Then they punished me again for not being upset that I was being punished."

When Ron was four years old, his parents decided to take him to the boys' club to learn how to swim. That gave them time to be alone on Saturday afternoons when Stanley didn't have to work. Their three other children were old enough to be left alone.

At that club no one wore bathing suits in the swimming pool, supposedly because thread and lint from the swimming trunks might clog the pool filter—hardly a valid reason. Ron's memory of the swimming lessons is fragmentary: "The memory that I have is not so much of being in the pool, but of being the last one getting out of the pool. I remember opening the door to the locker room, but the memory inside the locker room is blacked out. In its place, the emotion of rage takes over. Even in my adult years, the sight of naked males in a locker room or health club makes my blood begin to boil. Something awful happened behind that locker-room door. I'm not sure exactly what happened, whether it was actual sexual assault or just being humiliated because I was a vulnerable skinny little kid. Whatever form the abuse took, the shame of it haunted me for years!"

Ron had no real chums as a preschooler except for one little girl who was several years older than he. She lived in the neighborhood, and occasionally some of the kids would get together for a game of tag or hide-and-go-seek. Ron had fond memories of the little neighborhood chum. "I remember letting myself get caught, especially if it was by Nancy because then she would take me by the hand and put me in the circle for a time, and my whole body would shiver when she would hold my hand for a few seconds. I was so lonely; I so longed for gentle, nurturing touch, and I wasn't getting it at home. I would do most anything for the touch of someone whom I thought cared for me."

For some reason Stanley and Renata chose to have two more children after the war was over. Again, the children were not told of the impending birth of yet another sibling, so Ron had a shock one day when he came home from the movies to find a tiny baby brother in the old family crib. Enter Bobby. Ron noticed that Renata loved Bobby from the start. Stanley was home, and Renata did not fear Stanley's rejection because of this pregnancy. Then, in a couple of years, along came another new baby, this time a baby girl named Judith.

Renata had no help from the older children in caring for the two babies. Phyllis, who had cared for Ron from birth, was about to follow the lead of her older sister Peachy, who had already left home to marry Bill. Phyllis was fifteen and had been dating Johnny, who was likeable and friendly. Ron had taken to him well. It was no shock when Phyllis decided to marry Johnny, but it was devastating to seven-year-old Ron to lose the only mother figure he had known. George was gone. Peachy was gone. Phyllis would soon be gone, and Mother was totally consumed with raising a toddler and being pregnant again. Father, the one with whom he longed for a relationship, a friendship, a conversation, and acceptance, was totally preoccupied with supporting yet another new family and advancing his career.

Ron was alone again. There was no one to count on but himself. Somehow, he would have to survive—alone.

CHAPTER 4

Shortly after Bobby had arrived, life took a puzzling twist for Ron. He was sent away to kindergarten. Because he was used to solitary play, kindergarten was frightening and confusing. He often isolated himself from the other kids, busying himself with some solitary project. At least here toys and creative projects were available to occupy his time, and he flourished in the new environment in spite of not interacting with the kids around him.

Soon baby Judy arrived, and now both parents were consumed with caring for their needs, while Ron's needs or accomplishments went unnoticed and unacknowledged.

Membership in Cub Scouts provided another place of escape and a means of accomplishing something worthwhile. Little badges began to accumulate on his scarf, signs of accomplishment. Unfortunately, Renata and Stanley didn't regard Cub Scout events as important, and they neglected to attend the ceremonies at which badges and awards were distributed.

Ron quickly learned that money was important to his mother: She would notice him and praise him if he brought money home. It wasn't that they were so poor now; times had changed. But Ron so longed for her attention and praise that he lay awake nights dreaming up moneymaking schemes.

Ron had an idea! Toothpicks were inexpensive, but at first he used a few from the kitchen cupboard and sneaked Renata's cinnamon oil. He put a few drops of the oil on a piece of waxed paper and rolled the toothpicks in cinnamon oil. A new invention! Tearing a little piece of waxed paper off the roll, he placed five toothpicks in the paper and rolled it up, twisting both ends. Having made a few packets, he took them to school and to Scout meetings and sold them to the kids for a nickel. They went like hotcakes!

When Ron brought home the few nickels he had made, Mother was delighted and praised the boy. His projects grew from cinnamon toothpicks to short straws filled with Kool-Aid® and sugar. Instead of doing homework, he worked his trade, anything to be noticed by his mother.

Ron's grades in school never were very good, but no one at home seemed to care. School attendance was challenging for him because of the painful teasing he received from his classmates. He was teased in part because he was so skinny but primarily because he did not mix well with the other kids.

Tommy Mainville was his best friend. His sister was Nancy, the girl who made his heart leap whenever she touched his hand in outdoor games. They were next-door neighbors, and Ron and Tommy whiled away many hours in the tree house they had constructed. Tommy was the one friend Ron could trust, and together they shared secrets and dreams.

One summer morning Ron rang the neighbor's doorbell to get his friend to come out to the tree house, but Mrs. Mainville reported that Tommy was ill and couldn't come out to play. The next morning Ron was disappointed to get the same response again. A few days passed without the boys seeing each other, which was particularly tough on Ron since Tommy was his only real friend.

About a week had gone by since the boys had played together, and Renata offered Ron a quarter and suggested that he go to the movies. Bored and lonely, he sauntered off to the see the show and eat the few candies he could buy with the change. Ron took the long way home after the show, and as he turned the corner to his street, he noticed people and cars in front of his and Tommy's houses. It took him only a few moments to discover that the Mainvilles were in tears, and so were a lot of other strangers. Where was Tommy?

Ron's family always was expert at keeping secrets—not telling anyone what was happening. Soon Mrs. Mainville approached the bewildered boy and explained that he wouldn't be seeing his friend Tommy anymore. Tommy had been a "bleeder"—a hemophiliac—and had hemorrhaged to death a few days before. The funeral was over and the boy buried, and no one had bothered to tell Ron.

Ron climbed the rungs to the tree house, where he could cry alone and look down on the little garden that he had planted with Grandpa Miller. It seemed that Grandpa Miller was the only person left who cared about him. Ron had so many questions: Why were there no goodbyes? Why hadn't they told him the truth about Tommy's illness? Why did his parents always send him away? His best friend had vanished, and nobody at home cared enough to tell him.

The marigolds had peeked through the soil about a week before and grown to about two inches tall. Ron was sure that Grandpa Miller would be proud of the way he was caring for the little garden they had planted together. But thoughts of Grandpa Miller brought more questions: Where was Grandpa, anyhow? Why hadn't he come over to visit the last several weeks? Had Ron done something to upset Grandpa so he wasn't coming by to check on the marigolds? Ron had so many questions unanswered and no one to ask who would tell the truth.

One Saturday a few weeks later, Renata was rummaging around in the attic instead of baking as she usually did on Saturday mornings. Stanley called Ron to the garage where he was working and handed him a quarter to go to the movies. On Saturdays you could get two movies and a cartoon for the price of one. That was a good deal, but Ron was suspicious about why he was being sent away again.

Munching his last piece of licorice on his way home, Ron rounded the corner to his street, and there parked in front of his house was a huge truck. Phyllis, Johnny, Bill, Peachy, and Dad were carrying furniture toward the truck. They were moving! They couldn't move away and leave the garden! The marigolds were the only connection with Grandpa Miller, the only adult who cared! Ron's protests were met with Stanley's anger. "We're moving whether you like it or not. What's it matter? It's just a stupid little garden. You can plant another one at the new place. Now get in the car!"

The loaded car pulled away from the street, from the house, the tree house, and from Tommy's memory, and as the sight of it faded in the distance, a new determination was born in his young heart. Never again will I get close to anyone. I won't get hurt that badly again—never, never!

The new house on Wakasha Road was fancier than Ron had ever imagined. It was a sprawling ranch-style house, and it seemed to make Mother and Dad happy. Dad would sit in the breezeway on Sunday mornings with a cup of coffee, a cigarette, and the Sunday paper, while Ron was sent off to the local Lutheran church for Sunday School and services. The Sunday School part was OK, but the regular church service was boring to him. There he was, alone again. Stanley and Renata had given him that standard quarter for the offering, but he soon learned that he could sneak out of church for a bathroom break and use it to buy a wonderful milkshake at the corner store. That became his Sunday-morning treat for a long time.

Across the road from the house was an apple orchard; the owner lived a couple blocks away. Ron watched those apples ripen as he walked to school day after day and dreamed of an apple pie that he knew his mother could make out of the ones that had dropped to the ground. A high fence surrounded the orchard, and No Trespassing signs hung everywhere. Ron decided do the right thing. He would go to the neighbor and ask permission to pick up the windfalls.

When the orchard owner came to the door, Ron feared right away from the gruff way she said, "What do you want?" that she would refuse his request. He explained that Mother made wonderful pastries and asked if he could pick up the windfalls. "You stay out of that orchard, young man. If you touch one of my apples, I'll call the police and have you arrested. Do you understand?" she yelled. He understood all right, but he couldn't resist. Bringing home apples would be almost as good as bringing home money.

Mother had rolled out the crust for the apple pies she was making from the fruit he had brought her—a large brown bag of it—when the police drove into the driveway with the orchard owner. They were caught red-handed in the act of peeling those apples. The woman screamed and carried on for some time, but the boy was not arrested. Instead, Renata gave the woman a couple of dollars for the apples, and the problem was solved. On her way out the kitchen door, the owner called over her shoulder to Renata, "If the boy had just asked me for the apples, I would gladly have allowed him to pick up the windfalls."

In his family, children were to be seen and not heard, so Ron didn't even try to tell his side of the story. They wouldn't believe him anyway.

And the problem was only deepened by the neighbor's lie. She had lied about Ron, and it became very clear to him that day that the neighbor just couldn't be trusted.

Renata and Stanley spent Saturday evenings entertaining the neighbors and serving the pastries Renata had baked that morning. Before the neighbors arrived, she would grab Ron by his hair and drag him to his bedroom, where she would use a large skeleton key to lock him in. As friends came to socialize, Ron heard their laughter and believed it was directed at him because he was locked in his room. The smell of the coffee, and the knowledge that the pastries were disappearing without his being offered any, added to the resentment he was beginning to build toward all adults. Life was not fair. He was treated unfairly, and the pain was too much.

School became tougher for Ron, and no one was available to help. His behavior was adding to the scholastic difficulties, and frequently the "board of education" was broken while being applied to his backside. Ron didn't care. Truthfully, the pain felt good. At least at school somebody cared enough to give him the kind of attention that George used to get at home. "If I couldn't hit harder than that, I'd quit," Ron would tell the punishing teacher. The teacher would then beat him harder and longer because of the insults. He was becoming hardened and angry and found himself spending hours plotting revenge against those who had unjustly treated him.

Ron couldn't even count on long-term affection from his beloved pets. Blackie, his faithful black lab, had been shot one Saturday when he was sent to the movies. His cat, that had given birth to twelve kittens, mysteriously disappeared with her kittens another Saturday morning when he went to the movies. And his beloved rabbit, won at the theater, lay dead in its hutch when he returned from a Scout campout. Mother was supposed to be caring for the bunny, and she had let it die.

Stanley and Renata also neglected Ron by not attending his school plays or Scout functions, even though Ron excelled at Scout activities. Even the evening Stanley was to present Ron with the highest Scouting honor, Stanley didn't show up. The scoutmaster had to find a proxy to present the award to the boy. A perfect stranger placed the badge upon Ron that should have been his father's privilege and honor to do. Ron was still alone.

Ron added together all of his losses and injustices. He multiplied them by his inability to get the attention and affection of his parents, especially the father with whom he longed to relate. He piled on the humiliation he continued to suffer at school and the sexual abuse received two additional times before his teens—and he became a deeply hurt young man! Displaying pain isn't a manly thing to do, however, so Ron disguised his pain as anger, but not before trying to numb it with alcohol stolen from Dad's liquor cabinet.

His new "friends" were angry and fearless just like him. They were risk takers. Why not? When your life means nothing, when nobody cares, when you can't get an "I love you" or a "Good for you, Ron" from a parent, you figure that you must be really bad. It has to be about you, because they seem to love the brother and sister, just not you. What's the sense of worrying about your life if it's worth nothing? Just have fun!

And Ron and his pals did have fun. The greatest fun was creating gunpowder and bullets from scratch, making flaming arrows to shoot from willow-branch bows into passing semi trucks or the sides of barns. And there were the games of cowboys and Indians played with .22s and live ammunition, shooting at each other in the quarry. The more dangerous the game, the more excitement and challenge it brought, and Ron loved a challenge.

Rejected kids feel worthless. They become angry, sad, and fearful. Ron was all of these. Longing for a loving, affectionate father and the companionship of a role model and guide, and knowing he'd never have it, Ron crawled deeper inside himself, protecting the fragile child within from the rejection without. Without the perspective of an adult mentor, the future looked dim and the experiences of the past were exaggerated. Ron looked for and expected rejection from everyone he met, and usually he got what he predicted. The only satisfaction he got from life was pulling a destructive prank on some unsuspecting person or stealing enough money without getting caught to get the next bottle of numbness.

It was safer to be alone, away from the put downs and indifference at home, away from the teasing and torment of the other kids. Alone he could make money, spend it on liquor, and think his own self-destructive thoughts.

CHAPTER 5

Something was wrong with Renata. A rash had broken out on her arms and even a bit on her face. It itched terribly and drained a yellowish fluid. Her arms were wrapped in gauze bandages. The medication the doctor had prescribed made Renata so sleepy that she could hardly get out of bed. The ample supper the family expected became a matter of grabbing whatever Ron and Stanley could find for themselves and fix for the little ones.

Occasionally Phyllis, now with children of her own, would come out to the house and fix a meal for everyone, but that was a burden because she was pregnant again. Stanley's business was doing well, but something had to change because Renata was not getting better.

Finally, the doctors suggested that Stanley move away from Milwaukee to a different, less-stressful environment for Renata. Stanley entrusted his assets to a lawyer and began to look for a new location. No one knows why he chose North Little Rock, Arkansas, but Stanley and his brother-in-law decided to buy a motel business near there and run it together.

The details of that relocation and the subsequent financial mess are another one of the secrets that the family hid well. There was some kind of deceit going on with the lawyer in Milwaukee, and, for one reason or another, they never did buy the motel. Fortunately, Stanley was talented and had an excellent work record, making it easy for him to find another job, and soon he bought a gun repair and locksmith shop.

Across the street lived an older man who was a fanatic about the appearance of his lawn. He wanted all the blades of grass perfectly lined up and undisturbed. Ron remembers the experience this way: He was one of my customers on my paper route, and I delivered his paper just like I did everyone else's—on my bike. His front lawn was a gentle slope up toward the house, and I would throw the paper to the porch of the house as I passed by.

Well, that was not good enough for him! "You walk up the driveway and place that paper on my porch, young man. I don't want it thrown on the lawn!" he would bark. But after a while his constant chiding was annoying. No matter how I delivered his newspaper, he complained. So I made up my mind to take care of that old rascal.

I spent some of my paper route money and bought ten rocket fireworks.

I collected ten empty quart soda bottles and planted them in the vacant lot next to our house and pointed them all on an angle toward the house with the impeccable lawn. Carefully, I tied nine of the fuses together. Then I got a kid in the neighborhood to ring the old man's front door bell. When he came to the door, I let the single rocket go, and it landed right on his manicured front lawn. As soon as he tried to catch that rocket and stop it from hurting his grass, I lit the other nine. They went speeding right to the front lawn, and the poor man was in near hysteria trying to catch them all.

From that incident, I learned then that I could intimidate others and prevent them from bullying me. I had learned a lot in the Boy Scouts, and, applying that to what I had learned from some of the thugs I had palled around with, I became threatening enough to discourage the bullies who had plagued me before.

Something new was happening in my relationship with my father. He had taken a little interest in me and had promised to teach me how to spell. It seemed to irritate him that I couldn't get good grades in that subject, so he decided to drill me in the evenings. He said that the only reason I was passing in school was that he was paying off my teachers to pass me. I doubted that he was really telling me the truth, but the concern, whatever the reason, was a welcome change.

Often after school, I would go to the locksmith shop and work with him for a while until it was time to come home for supper. There I learned a lot of information that would come in handy in fostering my criminal behavior later on. One evening Dad asked me if I wanted to drive the truck home. I was fifteen and had no license, but Dad must have assumed that as long as he was supervising it was permissible. I was thrilled!

I remember thinking that night as I went to sleep that Dad and I were getting close. He actually sat near me in the cab of the truck on the way home. And he even told me that I had done a good job driving. I was really enjoying this new relationship!

My sixteenth birthday came and went on October 1, just like every other birthday had come and gone. I had no party, no cake, no presents, no singing—just another day in the week. My birthday had always been uncelebrated except for the year I turned twelve. All of the kids at school always had birthday parties, so I decided to create one of my own. I invited six or seven of the kids from school to come to the house at a certain time. With money I had saved, I bought a birthday cake and some soda. When my Dad came home from work, we were all sitting around the dining room table eating the cake. Dad began screaming expletives at the top of his lungs and demanded that all the kids go home. They were petrified, and so was I! They scattered, leaving behind the cake and the unopened presents they had brought.

After a ferocious lecture and much pounding of the dining room table, Dad demanded that I take the unopened gifts back to the kids who brought them. Talk about disappointment and embarrassment! Dad's reaction taught me that birthdays were better ignored. Just let them pass by, say nothing, and nobody gets hurt—nobody but me. And it doesn't matter if I get hurt, because I don't matter.

Only a few weeks later Stanley had the fatal heart attack (described in chapter 1). I remember waking up the morning following Stanley's death to the sound of women's voices in the kitchen. The neighbors had heard the ambulance and had come for more information. One of the neighbor women saw me come into the kitchen and must have felt that I looked out of place. She came to me, gave me a bit of a hug, and put a dollar in my hand. "Why don't you go to the movies, Ron? You don't need to be around all of this," she said. There it was happening again. I was being sent away, but this time not to avoid truth but to avoid pain.

Again I was sent away to sit in a theater, but this time I couldn't escape the present moment. In the darkness, I felt a wide range of emotions. One moment it was an incredible sadness because my hope of ever having a father had now vanished. The next it was fear for the future. What would it hold now that there was no one to earn a living for Mother and us three kids? I was sure that I could survive on my own, but what about Judy and Bobby? Before long, the truer emotion surfaced. I was angry! I was angry with my dad for dying just when we were beginning to build a relationship for the first time—but I was also angry at my mother. Why had she done this to me? Perhaps she was jealous that Dad and I were beginning to build a relationship. That must be it; she was jealous. Would she kill her own husband just to keep me away from him? Why didn't she kill me instead? I would rather have been dead than have to deal with her now. She had killed everything that ever was important to me: my dog, my bunny, the cat and her kittens, and now my dad! She had certainly killed any love I may have had for her before. She'd better not think that I'll be around for her, to be the head of the house. Never!

Coming out of that theater, I walked right by the candy counter. I had better things to do with my money. I needed a newspaper! Under the big bridge across the Arkansas River I read the truth; Stanley was dead.

When I arrived at the house, I was relieved to find Phyllis and Johnny and their kids were on their way from Milwaukee. Now I didn't have to be in charge. They must have literally flown from Milwaukee to get there so soon, but however they got there, I was glad to see them. When they were around, they made a safe place for a troubled kid, and I was that!

They left the next day and headed for Milwaukee with Bobby and Judy in their car. I stayed behind with Mom, to lock up the house and drive her to Milwaukee, where Dad would be buried. The thought of what the next few days would hold sent chills through me—funerals, graves, crying people, and a dead father. Mother expected me to drive the Cadillac to Milwaukee. I wondered how I could endure such a long trip with her. She sat in the front seat, lost in a daze, so somehow the drive went well until it was evening. Then she instructed me to pull over at a motel we were approaching. She sent me in with money and told me to get a room. The only room still available had only one bed, but that was OK. I didn't mind sleeping on the floor.

Mother changed into her nightgown and instructed me to get into the bed with her. I was appalled at the thought of sharing a bed with my mother. But I got in. She had taken some pills the doctor had prescribed, so I figured that she'd soon be asleep. As soon as I detected a change in her breathing, I rolled off the edge of the bed I'd been clinging to and took my pillow with me onto the floor. There I felt safe and comfortable and soon fell asleep.

The funeral itself was a blur. The pain and guilt I harbored for letting my father die in my arms reinforced by poor self-concept. The overwhelming devastation made me want to begin fulfilling the bargain I had made with God. My Dad had to be taken to heaven; I had to see to that.

Mother and I stayed in Milwaukee at Phyllis and Johnny's house for a while. Then the house in Arkansas had to be emptied and sold and our belongings brought back to Milwaukee. As usual, Phyllis and Johnny were our lifesavers. Looking back, I wonder how they managed to treat us so well. They had children of their own, jobs, and a life to live, but we had just been dumped on their doorstep, and Mother acted as if they were responsible for our keep.

It was at this point that my drinking escalated, and I was in so much pain that I didn't care who I hurt. I slept in an unfinished upstairs room, and night after night, I would come in late and drunk and attempt to climb that stairway to the second-floor bedroom where the four of us slept. But I was so inebriated that I would climb up three or four steps and fall back down again. I wakened the entire household, but I didn't care! I had given up caring, if I'd ever cared at all.

I worked at odd jobs here and there, trying to make enough to help the budget at home but being careful to keep enough money for the booze I needed to dull my pain. The odd jobs didn't pay enough to buy the alcohol I needed. That's when I began to steal money from any place I could in order to have money for liquor. I had a girlfriend, too, and I felt responsible to pay for some of her liquor. I spent long hours away from home, often at Joan's place, where her mother drank freely and they offered liquor to me. Life at that time was a blur of various levels of inebriation. Joan's acceptance boosted my damaged ego, and when I was with her, I had the illusion of meeting my need for closeness.

Scrapes with the law became commonplace, and before long I found myself standing before a judge who was determined to make me pay for the things I'd done. I was given a choice: I could go to the juvenile detention center, or I could enlist in the armed forces. I chose the navy. There I could see the world, escape from any responsibility to Mother and the kids, and become a man.

While it was hard to say goodbye to Joan, the prospect of "living life on the edge" in the navy was exciting. As the bus pulled out of Milwaukee heading for the Naval Training Station at Great Lakes, it felt as if I was leaving behind all my worries and my pain. I could picture myself coming back in my uniform, and beautiful Joan would be proudly waiting for me at the station! And perhaps Johnny, the man Phyllis had married, the only father figure I had, would be proud too. That's what really mattered!

CHAPTER 6

Boot camp reminded me of the Boy Scouts. There were regular meals and lots of rules, but somehow the whole thing revitalized me. Just as in Scouts, it felt like someone was watching out for me and caring about my decisions and accomplishments. I suppose it was the way I imagined a father would behave if he really cared about his son and wanted to see him succeed. Because the leaders at the base wanted me to succeed, I wanted to please them.

I did very well during those months of rigorous training. I felt proud to wear the navy uniform, just as I had been proud to wear the Boy Scouts' scarf with all its symbols of my success. Even though life at boot camp went well for me, in the evenings I would sneak several drinks to numb the pain of loneliness and failure I still felt. I would buy the alcohol off base and sneak it onto the base undetected. I was never caught while in Great Lakes.

The time came for graduation, and we sent invitations to family and close friends. I pictured myself receiving my diploma from boot camp with only the guys in my platoon to applaud. But when the day came, I was shocked to be called to the gate to welcome visitors. Phyllis and Johnny had brought my mother and Joan. I was thrilled, but was reluctant to show the emotion. After the ceremony, we went out to eat and then drove home to Milwaukee.

The few days we were allowed to be "home" before shipping out were filled with Joan, booze, and fun. As soon as we arrived in Milwaukee, I abandoned the family and went home with Joan. And that's where I stayed for those days of liberty—there, and at the nearby bar.

I was shipped out first to Norfolk, Virginia, and assigned to the *USS Fremont* APA-44, anchored in the harbor. Ship maintenance and mundane duties filled my days, and alcohol numbed the pain of my loneliness at night. Life in the navy was proving to be rather boring, and I longed for someone familiar, someone to care, and a little excitement. Since I had never been one to mingle with peers much, I was anxious for each leave and opportunity to visit Milwaukee.

Finally, the *USS Fremont* was going to set sail. Finally, I was going to see the world. The first few days at sea were without incident; the sea was calm and the work was routine. But after only a few days I was to experience my first storm at sea and some of the excitement that I craved. The bow would sink in the water until I thought that it would never come up again, and then the stern would sink. Waves crashed against the side of the ship, and I was both scared and sick. I was not the only one with a queasy stomach; the deck was covered with seasick sailors.

During one gigantic storm, I was on KP duty, preparing eggs for breakfast. Several thousand men on a ship require a lot of scrambled eggs, and we were cracking the raw eggs into a huge stainless steel mixing bowl that sat on the floor. Suddenly, the ship took a giant roll, and that heavy bowl of eggs slid across the kitchen floor and slammed into the far wall. Eggs flew everywhere, and now the rolling kitchen was made doubly treacherous by the slippery raw eggs sloshing around on a steel deck.

Of course we sailed in calm weather too. One night when I was on watch, I walked out onto the bow of the ship. The sea was sparkling in the light of a full moon. The ship cut through the glass-smooth ocean, and occasionally a dolphin would leap out of the water at the bow. I have never forgotten the peacefulness of that night and the feeling that came over me. All was right with the world at that moment, and if I could have died then, I would have been happy to be buried in the beauty I saw that night. I felt close to God there and had a taste of heaven.

Tangier, Morocco, was one of our ports-of-call on this tour. With another sailor I took my leave time to explore the port city and take in some of the local color. I was fascinated by the appearance of the Moroccan women. Only their eyes showed above a black scarf wrapped over their nose and mouth. With a few drinks under my belt, I became fool-hardy and courageous. As my pal and I walked past a Moroccan woman, I reached out and pulled down her scarf. Instantly, I heard a man holler and saw him racing out from a pub. He reached for his sword, pulled it from its scabbard, and then took off running after me, shouting in Arabic. I sprinted down the street, with the man close behind. Once, he lunged at me with his sword, and it wasn't until we were safely in another pub, having outrun him, that I saw the split in the back of my uniform. That was a close call!

I was drunk nearly all of the time. The other sailors on board could not figure out how I could be, considering that alcoholic beverages were not allowed on board ship. I had become adept at sneaking liquor onto the ship and to my hiding place and equally adept at stealing the money to buy the stuff.

One day while on duty on the gun deck, we were practicing the routine for firing the 40 mm guns. I loaded them in the manner in which I had been taught, but, by some fluke, one of the shells didn't fire and was tossed out onto the deck. One of the team yelled "live shell!" and we all jumped over the edge of the gun-turret shield. In the panic of the moment, I jumped off the wrong side and fell two decks to a steel deck below, where I landed on both feet and turned my ankles. The way I landed caused the ligaments to be torn at my ankles and both swelled immediately. Several X-rays later the ship's doctor told me that I would probably end up in a wheel chair because the damage was severe and not repairable.

I was in bed for a few weeks with both legs in casts but soon became restless. I begged for walking casts, which I got, and later was given half casts, which were held in place with ace bandages so they could be removed. In spite of the pain, I removed the half casts occasionally so I could go dancing. One evening I was seen on the dance floor by an officer. The next morning my casts were confiscated, and I was returned to normal duties.

The pain from that injury was intense, but with the prescription pain medication and the booze I had stashed away, I survived well. This new feeling that came from alcohol and pills combined gave me a whole new outlook on life. I was high and loved the feeling! When I felt like this, the feelings of loneliness, sadness, and total rejection were lightened, and I could survive.

At last, however, my foolish behavior to supply my addiction caught up with me, and I was in deep trouble. I was hauled off to the brig for having stolen money from the ship's store. There I was, facing a general court-martial and the humiliation of a dishonorable discharge from the navy. Behind bars and without the liquid drug I had come to depend on, I was at the end of my rope. The emotional pain surfaced again. I was alone and felt unwanted, unloved, rejected, abused, accused, and I wanted to die.

The storekeeper on board ship was a sailor named Charles E. Ward. I had never met him; I had just taken money from his store when he'd locked it up for the night. Charlie went to the commander of the *USS Fremont* and asked for an audience. In that meeting, he asked for me to be released into his custody. The request was unheard of. No commander in his right mind would release a prisoner to an enlisted man! But somehow Charlie's persuasiveness won out, and the commander came to unlock the brig.

"I'm releasing you into this guy's custody, Rockey, and I'm telling you it won't take much to have you returned right here to the brig for good. You follow Charlie everywhere he goes. When he eats, you eat. When he goes to the head, you go. When he goes off the ship, you go, but don't you let him lose you for one second! You got it, Boy?"

"Yes, Sir, I've got it. I'll stick right with Charlie, Sir. I sure will!" I told him. And we left the commander standing there as I followed Charlie from the brig to the ship's store.

Charlie was a quiet sort of a guy, a steady-Eddy. He was maybe a year or two older than I was. You could always count on him to do whatever he said he would do. And you could count on me to stand beside him while he was doing it. He had a red book that he read a lot, and once in a while he showed me the pictures. They were kind of scary drawings of beasts and dragonlike things, and I couldn't understand why in the world someone mellow like Charlie would be interested in that.

He never preached at me, but once in a while he would tell me that pork or bacon weren't good for me; so if Charlie didn't eat it, I didn't either. I was his shadow and followed him everywhere he went and did whatever he was doing. My bunk was changed so that mine was next to his, and I noticed that at night before he went to sleep he'd usually read his Bible and kneel beside his bed to pray. I didn't follow his lead there because God was a stranger to me and, anyway, He and I had made a bargain. I was on my way to hell so my Dad could go to heaven, so I'd better not get chummy with the man upstairs. That would defeat my purpose.

We were on our way back to Norfolk, Virginia, and about four days out of port, when the ship's list for two-week leaves was posted. I checked the list and found that I was in the third group for leave. In other words, I'd be waiting a month for leave, and Charlie was on the first-leave list. I wondered how this would work if Charlie wasn't on board ship for me to shadow, but I wasn't surprised to find my name on list number three. I knew full well that Charlie was deserving of the first leave and I, the last.

The day before we were to arrive in Norfolk, a revised list came out. My name had been moved, and I was scheduled for first leave and Charlie for the last. Charlie had taken my place—given up his leave for me. WOW! What a guy!

I packed my duffle bag and was on the deck waiting my turn on the gangplank when Charlie grabbed the duffle bag and said, "I'll carry your bag to the bus, Ron." Hoisting the bag over his shoulder, Charlie pushed me ahead of him toward the gangplank. We walked along in silence, probably because, for once, I was speechless. What do you say to a fellow like this who keeps giving up privileges for you?

We arrived at the bus stop ahead of time, and Charlie asked me how much money I had for my leave. I told him that my twenty dollars was enough. He reached into his pocket and pulled out eighty dollars—an entire month's pay—and handed it to me. "You take this," he said, "and if you have it when you get back, you can pay it back; and if not, it's OK." I think that I thanked him, but somehow I couldn't believe the kindness of this fellow who had just, out of the blue, taken me under his wing. What was this about? The bus pulled up to the curb, and I let the other guys on ahead of me while I just stood there not knowing what to say.

It was at last my time to get on the bus, and as I climbed the three steps Charlie called to me. "Ron, if you ever get in trouble, find a Seventh-day Adventist minister." The door closed, and I waved good-bye to this man I could not understand. What I did know about Charlie was that he was about my age and just an enlisted man, like me. I knew that he liked to read, that he prayed regularly, and that for some reason he cared about me. He had the attributes of a loving and compassionate father—the one for whom I had always longed.

CHAPTER 7

The thought crossed my mind as I rode away from the *USS Fremont* that Charlie had said goodbye as if he were not going to see me again. What a strange farewell. I rehearsed his words: "If you ever are in trouble find a . . ." If I am ever in trouble? Trouble followed me the way I had been following Charlie.

I was on my way home, and that's what counted. But where was home? I didn't have one, really. I had no father. Mother was still living with Johnny and Phyllis, and even though they always welcomed me and Phyllis would go out of her way to fix good meals, I always felt like we were all intruding. It just didn't seem fair to be barging in on their life just because Dad had died. Why did we have to make that their burden?

For me, going home was returning to Milwaukee, the city of my significant growing-up years. It was also being with Joan. As I look back at it now, I can see that we both were a mess. Both of us were rejected kids, and we both so longed to connect that, even though the relationship felt awkward at times, I stuck with her. We are attracted to those who are our emotional equals, and she was mine. Joan didn't have a father, either, well, not much of one. He was an alcoholic. Her mother was also a heavy drinker who frequented the local bars and would go home with anyone who would take her. Obviously, their marriage was a sham.

Years later, I wonder how I could have allowed her to have both Louis and me on the string at the same time. When I was around, I had her. When Louis was around, he had her. That lack of loyalty is what we saw at the bars. Couples would come in together and leave the bar with different partners. I hadn't been taught anything about relationships, so I didn't know better.

During this home leave, Joan got a call from Louis, who had been out to sea on maneuvers. He was calling from Bremerton, Washington, and wanted Joan to go there to be with him. I offered to accompany her; and then Joan, her mother, and I decided to go together in her mother's car. We got as far as Denver and ran out of money. The only thing that I could think to do was to call Charlie, who was on board the *USS Fremont* in Norfolk harbor.

When Charlie came to the phone, I told him that I was AWOL and needed money to get back to the ship. The answer he gave was not the one I wanted, but he was so convincing that I decided to follow his advice. He told me that in the city where I was, there was an air force base. I was to go there and tell them that I was AWOL from the U.S. Navy and was overdue back at the *USS Fremont* in Norfolk. Charlie told me that they'd take me in, feed me supper, give me a clean place to sleep and shower, and put me on a plane first thing the next morning back to the *USS Fremont.*

I abandoned the two women and went to the base. Charlie's advice was correct. They did just as he had said. However, the next morning after breakfast, and before I was to be flown to Virginia, I snuck off of the base and back to the motel where Joan and her mother were staying. Somehow, I couldn't let Joan go to Louis by herself. When I arrived at the motel, I discovered that Joan's mother had gone out to a bar the previous night and later returned to the motel with enough cash to drive herself back to Milwaukee and to put Joan and me on a bus to Bremerton.

Louis acted pleasant enough when he saw us together, and we decided to go to a bar for a few drinks. While I got up off the barstool to put a quarter in the jukebox, Louis poured carbolic acid in my drink. We sat there for a couple of minutes, and Louis said that he'd rather go to a different bar. "Drink up, Ron," he said, "and let's split." I downed my shot glass full of what I thought was a mint drink and slid off the stool to leave but staggered only as far as the end of the bar, where I collapsed.

The next thing I knew I was awakening in an intensive care unit of a hospital. I'd been there unconscious for three days. That I still had a throat and stomach was a miracle! The carbolic acid had eaten a hole in my stomach, and I had nearly hemorrhaged to death. Because I was in uniform when I had passed out, I had been taken to the naval hospital. It was quickly determined who I was, that I was AWOL, and that I was going nowhere at all until this gaping wound had healed.

Furthermore, the medical personnel thought that I had attempted suicide, that I had swallowed the carbolic acid intentionally, so they assigned me for a few weeks to the psychiatric ward. I knew the truth—that Louis had tried to kill me—but I refused to tell the story to the doctors. I didn't want to get Louis in trouble, and I figured that since I couldn't prove Louis's actions, it would be his word against mine if it came to an inquiry. To be honest, I was protecting Joan too.

Those few weeks locked in a psychiatric ward with mentally-ill inmates, just hanging around doing nothing, was almost more than I could take. A small amount of time was devoted to therapy, but most of the time I just watched TV or listened to ranting or screaming patients. I finally decided that I had to leave. The time I had spent in Dad's locksmith shop helped me to form a "key," which I used to open one of the locked windows every night for several nights. It didn't take long for the authorities to figure out who was opening the window, so they finally discharged me, as I had hoped they would.

After my hospital discharge, I was restricted to the naval base in Bremerton for sixty days and then reassigned to the *USS Paul Revere,* whose homeport was San Diego. Even though I had enjoyed the challenge of basic training, I was miserable in the navy. I felt too confined aboard ship, so when it came time for my next liberty, I returned to Milwaukee to look for Joan. I overstayed my liberty time again and still had not found her. A friend of my brother heard that I was AWOL again and determined to help me. He found me at the local hangout, trying to drown my pain the only way I knew. With a gun stuck in my ribs, he walked me out of the bar and into his car. At gunpoint he and his girlfriend drove me downtown to the navy recruiter and made me turn myself in. They sent me to Great Lakes Naval Training Center, and once again I landed in the brig for a time and then was restricted to base.

I had been in the navy for two years. I had seen more than I cared to of the world at that point. Confused, lonely, rejected again by a woman, and physically depleted, I longed for something, someone, anything but the restrictive navy. The guys on base saw how miserable I was and teased me about getting out of the navy. I responded by bragging that I could get out within sixty days—with an honorable discharge. Of course they bet me that I couldn't.

I had always loved a challenge, so suddenly I came alive. I won the bet; and less than sixty days later I left the Great Lakes Naval Training Center, where I had started my navy career, and I left the United States Navy.

I never saw Louis or Joan again.

Sometime after I left the *USS Fremont,* my mother received a letter from Charlie. In it Charlie told her that she should not worry about me; instead, she should just pray for me. He told her that God had His hand "on your boy, and He will never let him go." The letter was typewritten, and Charlie's name was typed at the end. There was no signature.

Through the years there have been people who, having heard the story of Charlie's consistent love and caring, have offered to find Charlie. They have searched old records of the church to which he was supposed to have belonged; they have hunted through naval records, and they have left no stone unturned in the search for Charlie. They have even looked at a copy of the *USS Fremont's* manifest, and there was no Charles E. Ward. He is a man to whom I owe a great debt of gratitude, but he seems to have vanished without a trace. Was he an angel?

Now I had a new question to ask myself: What would I do with the rest of my life? I had quit high school in the second semester of the ninth grade. The US Navy had forced me to take a GED test, which I did begrudgingly, just checking answers randomly, and, for the most part, not reading the questions. I did have a GED diploma. I had no career and no intention of going to any kind of a school to prepare for one. I did know something about locksmith work and a bit about heating and air-conditioning, but that was it.

For no logical reason, I decided to hitchhike to Memphis, Tennessee. Why I chose that section of the country I do not know. I had no desire to go to Milwaukee because Joan wasn't there. My mother and younger brother and sister were still living with Phyllis and Johnny, and I didn't want to add to their burden. I had decided that I wanted to be a dancer because the good dancers were able to attract good-looking women; so I enrolled in classes at Arthur Murray's dance studio. One thing I had going for me as a dancer was that I had natural rhythm. My experience of playing the drums in the navy band had helped develop that ability.

Because I advanced so rapidly, I was soon hired on at the Arthur Murray Dance Studio as a ballroom dancing instructor. The old saying is that practice makes perfect, and I am convinced that in my case it was true. I danced every day, except Sunday, from ten o'clock in the morning until well after midnight. When the instructing was over for the day at 9:00 P.M., the other instructors and I would go to a club to dance some more. I would consume a drink between each dance, and finally, by the time the club was closed for the night, I'd have a hefty bar tab. I drank most of my paycheck and still had room and board to pay at the boarding house where I lived. In order to survive, I went back to conniving how I would get more money. I was able to sneak from the till at the dance studio, and occasionally a wealthy student would give me a sizeable tip.

As I look back on it now, I recall the joy that I derived from really being a help to my students, and, even then, I was preparing for a life much different from the one I was living. One of my students was a woman in her sixties who had been a victim of polio. She had heard that dancing would be the kind of exercise her weakened legs needed, and, if successful, she might be able to give up her braces and crutches forever. It was exciting to see her dream become a reality and to have the privilege of hanging her crutches on the studio wall, never to be used by her again. I had bright moments of happiness when I could help people achieve their goals.

All the while I was as sick emotionally as that woman with polio had been physically. My only method of surviving the rejection, which had become my identity, was to stay so inebriated that I was numb to the pain that plagued me when sober. And in order to maintain numbness, I had to steal. It's only a matter of time before your vices catch up with you, and I was about to be captured by the local police. Too much money had been missing from the till, and I feared that the manager would suspect his star employee.

One of the other instructors had recently left the studio to enter the ministry, so when I announced that I was leaving also, the others asked if I was going to follow suit. Incredibly, the thought had crossed my mind once or twice, but I would laughingly dismiss it as the craziest notion ever. And that's exactly what I did as I was leaving employment at Arthur Murray.

Only a few hours had passed, however, before I was arrested. I had been stashing some money in a bank account, and before leaving town,

I went to the bank to withdraw it. I was only nineteen, and the teller thought it strange that such a young fellow would have so much money to withdraw. I'm not sure what their procedure was, but the bank notified the police, and before I could turn around, I was in handcuffs. Of course it was discovered that this was the money missing from the dance studio.

I was sentenced and taken to the Shelby County Correctional Facility. There I was, a Yankee in a Southern prison, and if anyone was going to be tortured, I soon found out that it would be me. There every prisoner had a work detail, and I was assigned to the crew that made cement bridge abutments. It was summer, and the Tennessee sun can wreak havoc on a fellow with very fair skin. Everyone was to work in shorts with no shirts. My job was to push a wheelbarrow up a narrow plank and dump the full load of cement into the bridge forms. The guards carried whips and shotguns and warned us that if we spilled a load of cement, we would pick it up with a teaspoon.

By the end of the first day, I was beet red and feverish and nauseated from the sunburn. My hands were so swollen that they would not close. I slept by soaking my towel in cold water, wringing it out, and laying it along my body. Two or three times in the night I resoaked the towel and laid it on me again.

By morning my entire body was swollen. My face was so puffy that my eyes were just slits. I asked permission to go to the infirmary, hoping that they would allow me to stay indoors, but the guard's response to my request was, "Shut up, Boy, and get in line!"

When I got outside, a fellow whom I thought was one of the guards offered me something that would help my burn and stop it from getting worse. What he gave me was motor oil, and I applied it lavishly, not realizing that it would cook my skin.

The following night was sleepless. No amount of wet towels could ease the pain, and my hands were so swollen that I couldn't wring out the towels. The next morning I asked again to go to the infirmary and was given the same answer as the day before. However, this time I broke line on the way to breakfast and went to the infirmary. The doctor there gave me a three-day indoor pass and told me to present it to the guard.

Of course the guard was incensed! "Well, if it's indoors you want, Boy, we'll gladly give it to you! Come with me." I was taken to solitary confinement, locally known as "the hole." It was that, for sure, a 4' x 6' x 6' cold, damp box. Before entering, I was stripped of my clothes. There was no furniture and no lavatory facilities. The food was equally disgusting! We would get tin bowls of maggot-infested rice and stale bread twice a day. I was there until the guard was good and ready to let me out. It was several weeks, but I don't know the precise length of time.

At that facility each Saturday there was a "warden's call." That meant that you could go to the warden with your complaints or grievances, and he would listen. It was not guaranteed that he would do anything about your problem, but he would listen. So on the first Saturday after I was out of "the hole," I signed up to see the warden. I will guess that he was about five-and-a-half feet tall and weighed perhaps four hundred pounds. He sat behind his desk, and his belly protruded so far that he set his 38-caliber gun on top of it. He was chewing tobacco, and the slimy, brown juice slobbered down his jowls. Every couple of minutes he'd spit into a spittoon.

Speaking as if he had a few too many drinks, he asked, "What-do-you-want, Boy?"

"Well, Sir," I said boldly, "the guards are torturing me. If you don't get them off my back, I'm going to leave."

Spitting again, the warden chuckled. "Well, Boy, nobody's ever 'scaped from this here place. (spit) If you thinks you can leave, you go right ahead." (spit)

I had my permission, so all I needed was my plan. By the next Friday, I was gone from there. I sneaked into the guard's locker room when they were busy, took a shower, and put on their aftershave and one of their uniforms. Since it was a misty evening, I put on one of their rain slickers and hat too. I found a crowbar in their supplies and shoved it up the sleeve of the raincoat, turned around with head lowered, waved at the guards in the towers, and they waved back. Then I closed the gate and was gone.

I look back at this today and wonder what I was thinking of. I do know one thing—my life in that Southern prison was worth nothing; I was doomed to be tortured. If they had caught me when I was in their locker room or fired at me when I was walking through the gate, it wouldn't have mattered to me. I was on a suicide, get-to-hell mission anyway, so I figured it best to take my chances. At that time I had no ties. As far as I was concerned, nobody wanted or loved me, I had no father, and I was nobody's son.

CHAPTER 8

It must have been during the busy commuter rush hour because the cable car was bulging with people. Groaning and inching its way up the steep hill, the old, wooden car finally came to the crest and made its regular stop. Quite a few passengers got off, and finally I could see the view! I stared for a few moments, and then I knew that I had to get out of San Francisco immediately!

Alcatraz Prison seemed to be staring back at me and gave me a sense of foreboding. From experience I knew that handcuffs were constricting, and Shelby County Facility was cruel. But I would rather be dead than be in Alcatraz! I was now an escaped prisoner and felt as though I wore a huge sign that read "Catch Me!" I was truly scared, and that was quite a change for me!

At the airport, I decided to escape to Hawaii. I had enough money left for a plane ticket and a couple of meals once I got there. Anxiously I awaited the plane's departure and the start of my new life.

Honolulu was crowded, an easy place to get lost, to hide, to be alone. Being alone in a new place did not bother me; I was used to being alone. It felt great to be free again, away from the barbarism of the Tennessee prison and the watchful eyes of fellow prisoners. I figured it would be easy to find employment in Hawaii. After all, I was a professional dancer—an Arthur Murray Gold Bar Instructor—and in a city like Honolulu, dancing had to be a favorite pastime of the tourists. I had my credentials from Arthur Murray, but I didn't want to work for them for fear that they might trace me back to Tennessee, and the police would pick me up in Hawaii. More than anything else, I did not want to land back in a Tennessee prison. So I applied and was hired on for a few months at a Fred Astair Dance studio.

At the dance studio I met a girl who took an interest in me. She was a student, and I dated her a few times. She was a kind person, and that kindness felt good for a while. When it was time for her to return home to Florida, I decided to go with her. By then I had saved enough money to make the trip and to pay for board and room until I could find work. She went on ahead of me to northern Florida, and I flew to Miami a few days later.

I really wanted someone all my own, someone significant whom I could love and who would love me, but all those in the past who were supposed to love me had betrayed me instead. Actually, I was not at all sure what love was. The only positive thing I knew of love was what I had seen in movies. The actors portrayed love and sex going together like bread and butter, so I assumed that I could get to love through sex. That assumption turned out to be an illusion.

The nightlife in Miami was even better than that in Honolulu. I stayed at a swanky hotel where there was dancing every night. One night a woman in her sixties asked me to dance with her, and we won the dance contest. She had been an Arthur Murray student so was adept at following and complementing the style I was used to. I really enjoyed the partying and the admiration of fellow dancers those few days and decided to stay in Miami longer than planned. I was living it up, dancing every night and living like a king. I hadn't forgotten the girl, but in Miami I was enjoying even more receiving the attention of several people at one time.

In order to continue living the high life, I needed more money than I could make teaching dancing. Where this idea ever came from I'll never know, but I concocted a scheme to sell five hundred landing-craft boats to the Cubans. While in the navy I had been trained to pilot these specialized beach-landing boats, so I was familiar with them. This was during the time of J. F. Kennedy's presidency, and plans were being made to invade Cuba. Incredibly, I didn't have even one boat and had no idea how to get one. The method I would use to escape the angry Cubans I hoped to con wasn't formulated yet either. All I could think about was the money the scheme would bring in.

The outrageous idea presented a huge challenge to me, and I became addicted to the rush I felt as I endeavored to contact Cuban authorities. Of course, I did not envision the extreme danger I would be in if I came even close to pulling off this deal. Even if I had been able to comprehend the jeopardy in which I was placing my life, it wouldn't have made a difference once I had begun. To be able to pull off such a grand scheme would have made my ego soar, and that was all I thought about. I did not realize then that I compensated for my early rejection with the ability to imagine wild, grandiose schemes and often had the accompanying charisma to pull them off.

There was, however, a hitch in the plan; as I look back at it today, I see it as divinely appointed. What Charlie had said in the letter he wrote to my mother was true. God had placed His hand on me and was not going to let me go.

The Cuban maid who cleaned my room at the hotel was the one with whom I had made arrangements to meet officials to discuss selling them "my" boats. I had a nine o'clock morning appointment, and I was charged. I was able to sleep the night before only because I had knocked myself out with booze.

The phone rang in my room waking me from a sound night's sleep. It was the front desk providing my wake-up call so that I would have enough time to shower and dress for the important meeting. The voice on the phone said, "Good morning, Sir. It is eight o'clock on Friday the thirteenth and a beautiful day in Miami." Another bell rang inside my head. I was not a superstitious person, but the thought of having an important appointment on Friday the thirteenth rang an alarm. "Don't go," came the instruction in my mind.

So I hopped out of bed, put on my swimming trunks, and went out to the beach. A swim refreshed and soothed me, and I emerged from the water sure that I had made the right choice in breaking the appointment. After a few minutes in the ocean, I settled down on a lounge chair on the beach right in front of my hotel. Just as I was taking a sigh of relief, four men in business suits approached me and called my name.

Immediately they flashed FBI badges. They said that they wanted my identification, that the hotel was concerned because I had run up a large bill, and they didn't know how such a young kid could pay it. I told them that I had means to pay the bill and would prove that to them. Fortunately, I had brought my slacks and wallet with me, so I reached in the pockets of my pants and pulled out my wallet. There were only a couple of twenties in it and a pocket full of change in the slacks. I had friends in the dancing business who I was confident would wire me the money for the hotel, so I wasn't all that worried.

The agents walked with me to a phone booth, and I began to place the call. One of the agents started going through my wallet. As my friend answered the phone, I explained that I needed some money and was about to say where it should be wired when I noticed that the FBI agent had discovered my two sets of identification. I had one full set in my own name and another in my stage name. That was no problem except that I had two different draft cards, and that was illegal. When I saw the agent's eyebrows rise, I knew that I was in trouble again. I told my friend, "Forget it," and hung up the receiver.

In seconds I was slapped in handcuffs, taken to my room to get my things, and driven to the police station. It didn't take them long to discover that I was an escapee from the Shelby County Correctional Facility in Tennessee. I would be locked up now for sure!

Soon I stood before the judge in handcuffs. Nineteen years old, already with a record of numerous scrapes with the law and an escape to my credit, I was hardened and arrogant. Nothing mattered. I figured that my life was going according to plan—I was well on my way to taking my Dad's place in hell, as I had asked God to do for me. I was accomplishing the goal I had set for myself. I was becoming like my older brother George, and that, too, had been one of my plans. Once when I was about eleven, George had just come out of prison, and when he came home to visit Mother and Dad, I told him that I wanted to be just like him.

I had made my choice of a life of crime even before Dad died when I was sixteen. By that age I had been disappointed in people so often that I wanted to pay back somebody, anybody, for what had been done to me. I had been sexually abused three times by then, male to male, and the resulting rage was eating me alive! I look back now and see that I actually had a death wish, manifested in the daredevil behaviors that I was already into and the hair-raising risks that I regularly took.

After the judge listened to all the evidence, he asked me if I had anything to say. Boy, did I! My vocabulary was far worse than a drunken sailor (of course I'd already been one of those), and I gave it to the judge both barrels! I used every curse word in the books and then some. I told him all about the cruelty in the Shelby facility and boldly stated that I wasn't going back to that place! "Well," the judge said, "since you've stated your feelings so well, I'm going to do you a favor. I am sentencing you to the Youth Corrections Act."

When I got back to my cell, the other inmates asked how I had made out in court. "It pays off to tell the judge what you think, because he did me a favor. He sentenced me to the Youth Corrections Act."

The guys laughed hysterically. "Favor, my foot," one of them said. "You should have gotten only four years, and that judge just gave you six!" Oops! My big mouth had really gotten me into a mess this time, and there was no amount of charisma that was going to get me out of it.

Since having the two draft cards is a federal offense, I was taken to El Reno, Oklahoma, to the federal penitentiary. What a frightening place! Just the process of going through admissions is chilling! But I soon discovered that it was going to be a learning experience like no other I had ever had. One good thing was that the guards were nowhere near as cruel and caustic as those in Shelby County.

For thirty days I was kept, as are all newcomers, in the classification center and then transferred to a regular cellblock. During my time there I was employed as a typist, and because I was an industrious worker, I was asked if I would like to be taught photography and darkroom procedures. I jumped at the chance to learn something new and took to it easily. This was a creative job, and I felt like I had found my niche—in prison yet. During my time working in the photo lab, I had the privilege of developing all the photos taken of a famous escape from Alcatraz. After working on those photos, I knew for sure that my instincts to get out of San Francisco were accurate!

Federal prison also offered me the opportunity for a psychological work-up. Not only was I required to take tests, but also I chose to go beyond the testing to some individual and group work. Dr. William Menninger was my psychiatrist and the leader of the group therapy I attended. I do not know if they labeled me with a mental disorder or not, and, to tell the truth, it doesn't matter. I was introduced to Karl Menninger's book *The Human Mind,* and thus began my interest in learning what makes people tick, including myself. It would be, however, quite a while before the information would make an impact on my life. What was important was that I did learn a great deal in those group sessions, and that experience has benefited me greatly since.

In El Reno a man named W. B. Blanton was in charge of the classification center. I was magically drawn to him because of his kindness and the respectful manner in which he treated his prisoners. Mr. Blanton took me under his wing, taught me a great deal, counseled with me, and gave me every opportunity to improve myself in preparation for a life outside of prison walls. In short, his attention was the kind for which I had longed ever since Grandpa Miller had died.

I remember what he did for me the day I came out of solitary confinement. I had been bum-rapped. One of the prisoners who worked at the desk next to mine had hidden his "shiv" (knife) in my desk drawer, and it was found during a routine shakedown of the office. Of course, he did not confess, but Blanton and Caldwell, his assistant, knew that it wasn't mine. I paid the price for what the other con had done, and the price was two weeks in solitary and a demotion of work and living status.

The day I came out of solitary, Blanton requested me to return to the classification center to work. He and Caldwell called me into his office and closed the door. On his desk was a tape recorder, and Blanton pressed the play button. The tape recorder began to play a familiar tune, and the soloist began to sing:

Nobody knows the trouble I've seen,
Nobody knows my sorrow.
Nobody knows the trouble I've seen. Glory hallelujah!
Sometimes I'm up, sometimes I'm down,
Oh, yes, Lord.
Sometimes I'm almost to the ground,
Oh, yes, Lord.

Blanton stood listening to the words with Caldwell and me, and tears flowed down his cheeks. He knew I was innocent, but he had no way to help me escape the other prisoner's punishment. When the song ended, Blanton patted my shoulder. "I'll tell you what, Ron, I've never seen a prisoner take a bum-rap so gracefully. I am proud of you, Son."

Son? The word was beautiful music to my ears. He believed in me, and I decided that I would prove to him that I could rise above this injustice and become somebody again.

To the extent that prison can be a good experience, my time there was beneficial to me. Not only did I become proficient in taking and developing photographs, but I also learned how to take and classify fingerprints. More important, I began to learn a bit about myself. That's where my interest began in understanding how people think and why they act as they do.

Unfortunately, prison time was not over when I had served out my time in federal prison. The state of Tennessee awaited my arrival to finish the time I owed to them and to pay additional time for the escape. I dreaded the trip back to the hot and humid South and the torture that awaited me at Shelby. I had escaped from the place where "nobody escapes from," and I knew that when they got me back, the persecution would be gruesome. When the gates at El Reno opened, awaiting me on the other side would be officials from Tennessee. I wished that they would kill me on the spot rather than take me back to be brutalized again.

We rode to Tennessee by bus. I was handcuffed and shackled; the handcuffs were removed only long enough for me to eat a sandwich. I didn't bother to ask where the men were taking me. Trying to doze off to sleep was impossible. The pressure of the metal cuffs and shackles gave me a terrible headache, and riding in the back of the bus made me nauseated. Even as a child, I was always carsick when riding in the back seat, especially when my dad smoked cigars, and these guards smoked the entire trip to Tennessee. I fought the nausea, however, not wanting to anger the officers or the other cons.

Finally, the bus slowed down, and I could read the sign—Nashville State Penitentiary. We pulled into the long driveway, passed through the guarded gates, and pulled up in front of the place. It looked like a creepy castle. There were huge towers and far-as-the-eye-can-see walls. I noticed right away that the American flag was not flying, and the landscaping was stark. Not a flowering shrub or a colorful flower graced the grounds as they had in El Reno.

They unloaded the twelve of us off the bus and marched us, still shackled, single file into the back entrance, where all the new prisoners enter. Everything smelled of fresh paint, but everything was the same color—battleship gray. That was familiar from my time in the navy. What a sharp contrast to the place I had just come from! Huge steel doors clanged shut behind us, and with the sound came a revulsion for the place. It wasn't so much the building as it was that the building was in Tennessee, and I hated that.

Within moments we were in a locker room, and our shackles were removed. We were told to strip for a shower and a search. First we went to the showers, and for a few moments under the stream of the shower I felt free. The sound of the water and the clean-smelling soap I was using blocked out the nightmare of where I was, but all too soon the water shut off, and a towel was thrown at me. Each of us endured the humiliation of a rectal exam to check for contraband drugs or weapons. After that horror we were given sets of underwear and moved to another room.

There a guard announced that he was God. "We've got rules here, plenty of them, and you are gonna obey them or else. And in this place, I'm the boss. Things go my way. Now if there's any one of you punks who thinks he wants to be the boss, just step forward in line, and you and me will go in that there room, and we'll decide who's the boss."

Instantly, my anger flared, and the drive to challenge this guy was almost more than I could suppress. Just as I was about to step my right foot forward, another kid stepped out ahead of me. The guard said, "OK, Boy, go ahead to that room." We watched that kid go into the room and also watched the guard take a big ring of keys off his belt. When the kid turned around to face the guard, that ring of keys swung around and sliced open the side of his face. Blood spurted everywhere as he fell to the ground. What a feeling in the pit of my stomach! It could have been, and almost was, me on the floor. Nonchalantly, the guard stepped over him, replacing the keys on his belt, and picked up the telephone.

"Ya'll come on up here to the striping room and pick up this new kid. He just fell down the steps," the guard barked. Then he came back out to where we were standing in our skivvies and asked if anybody else wanted to be boss. No one moved. "Well then, Girls, get your clothes on, and we'll take you to your cell block. We dressed in the gray-and-white stripes known only too well as prison garb, with the numbers across our backs.

It didn't take too long to hear the story of the Nashville State Penitentiary from other prisoners. The reason that all the walls were gray, that the flag was not flying, and that there were no flowers or shrubs, was that there had been a riot a few weeks before. Apparently, the prisoners had rioted against the cruel and unusual treatment they were receiving and against the deplorable food they were being served. From what I heard, the riot was difficult to quell, and when the prisoners finally had been subdued, the guards decided to retaliate. They had pulled up all of the flowers and shrubs, painted the entire place gray, pulled down the United States flag, and brought all of the Bibles and other reading materials in the cells out to the center of the compound. There they doused them with gasoline and lit them on fire. The prisoners were going to get the message that challenging the authorities would get them even worse treatment.

There I was again, a Yankee in a Southern prison, in the state I had come to hate, in a prison with cruel guards, and personally in a state of panic. I had to find an escape route; I couldn't stay there! When I had bargained with God that I would go to hell in place of my dad, I thought one went to hell after one died. That's what I had agreed to in my mind. I didn't make any deal to live in hell during this life. My plan was to create hell for others!

CHAPTER 9

My cellmate was a tall, very black man. I felt comfortable with him because I had a special warm memory of Blacks. While I was a teenager living in Little Rock, my only chum was a Black kid who lived out in the woods. Occasionally he would take me to his house, and, invariably, his mom would invite me to stay for supper. They were poor, but that woman was a wonderful cook. She made the best fried chicken I'd ever tasted and the lumpiest, most delicious mashed potatoes ever!

I was always welcomed there, and I can remember wishing that I were her son. When I would call her Ma'am, as I always did, she would seem annoyed. One day she said to me, "Boy, don't you be callin' me Ma'am! I is a Black woman, and no White boys calls a Black woman Ma'am."

"Well I do," I said. "You are a Ma'am as far as I'm concerned, and I shall be calling you that."

Reuben was a quiet man. His tall frame was bent over from sitting on the bottom bunk and being too tall to sit up straight. He stood up and greeted me warmly when his cell door was opened and I was shoved in. We didn't speak too much for the first few days. I had a lot of thinking to do. Mainly, I was trying to plan an escape route. I just couldn't settle down until I'd figured out how to get out. That kind of confinement was nearly impossible for me to handle without cracking up.

When we did begin to talk, to share with each other our backgrounds and the reasons for our incarceration, I learned that Reuben had been sentenced to prison for ninety-nine years. He was serving the time for killing his wife and child, but Reuben was not a violent man. Somehow, I could not picture this man hurting anyone.

He had been overseas during the Korean conflict, fighting for his country. When his time in the service was up, he came home unannounced to surprise his wife, but when he got to their house, she was in their bed with another man. Reuben was devastated, grief-stricken. They had two children, and Reuben couldn't fathom how his wife could betray him. His hurt turned immediately to rage, and, since rage has no sense, he went to the garage, got the gas can, poured gasoline around the house, and lit up the place.

While it was burning, he heard his daughters screaming inside the inferno. In his great disappointment, he had forgotten that his girls would be in the house too. He went in to save them, but was able to save only one of the two children, and she was badly burned. His wife and her boyfriend died in the fire also.

Reuben was trying to forgive himself for what he had done. His little girls were both precious to him. There in the cell he had a tiny little picture of his daughters; crumpled from trying to hide it from the guards who would have confiscated that, too, when they tore all the reading materials from the cells. That picture was his prized possession and the only tangible reminder of what had been. His was called a crime of passion, motivated by love gone sour, by hopes dashed, and by commitments broken. It had left Reuben to suffer through the agony of the loss and the punishment for his crime. It had left a daughter to endure multiple surgeries to repair the damage done in his moment of agonizing pain. I understood after hearing the story that his stooped shoulders came not only from sitting on the lower bunk but from the load of guilt and remorse that was his to carry.

Reuben was a model cellmate. Right away he began to prepare me for what was to come from the guards and acquaint me with the way of the penitentiary. He was careful in his presentation, as I'm sure he could tell that this arrogant young cellmate of his was an I'll-do-it-my-way kind of kid. We were so different! I was the talker, the one with the filthy mouth; he was the listener, slow and gentle of speech. He listened well to me and sought to mellow this powerfully arrogant kid.

He had a wonderful command of the English language and often used words beyond my comprehension. He told me that, before the riot, he had both a Bible and a dictionary in his cell; every day he would learn one new word and its meaning. Then he would write and speak sentences using the new word he had learned. I saw him as a very intelligent man with a sensitive and loving nature. He was helping to make this dreaded sentence less painful by his kindness and the safety that his presence in the cell created. He was old enough to be my father, and the atmosphere around him was as safe as I understood a father's should be.

Outside the cell the prison was a hotbed of conflict. The older prisoners were still agitated that their uprising had not improved the conditions at all. The rumors stated that the kitchen help urinated in the coffee and vomited in the scrambled eggs. The food was swimming in pork grease, and everything tasted the same.

All prisoners had to line up to go to the cafeteria. We were allotted fifteen minutes to stand in line, get our food, eat our food, and get back in line. Prisoners were the ones working in the kitchen and serving the food. The rule was that you had to eat everything on your tray or you would be sent to the "hole," the infamous 4' x 6' x 6' cold, damp box. To torment the other prisoners, the servers would pile far too much food on your plate, just to see whom they could send to the hole that meal. It was quite a challenge to meet the requirements, and almost every meal one or two guys would be dragged off to their fate.

I became quite adept at finishing my food quickly—anything to avoid that dreaded "hole."

One day in the cafeteria line I saw on the bulletin board a new notice. It read, "Seventh-day Adventist Church Services—9:00 A.M. Saturday in the chapel." As I inched along slowly in line, I began to wonder why that notice struck a familiar chord. Where had I heard something similar before? It wasn't until I was seated at the table and halfway through my lunch that it dawned on me where I had heard those words before. Charlie. Charles E. Ward. He had spoken those words as I got on the bus to go on home leave. "If you ever get in trouble, find a Seventh-day Adventist minister."

I was in trouble, to be sure! I was a prisoner in Tennessee, confined in a battleship-gray castle with no light of day penetrating those thick stone walls. I was a hated Yankee in a Southern prison with the threat of the "hole" above my head every moment of every day, it seemed. If I ever needed help, I needed it then.

"I should go and see what Charlie was talking about," I thought. "Tomorrow is Saturday, so when the guards are putting us back in our cells, I'll ask to go to church in the morning."

As the cell door was about to close, I spoke to the guard. "Sir, I'd like to go to those church services in the morning—the Seventh-day ones," I said.

"You ain't going to no Advent services, Boy. You're a Catholic."

"Sir, I am not a Catholic," I said, "and I really want to go to church tomorrow morning."

"Well, you've been going to the Catholic services, and you ain't going to no Advent stuff. You think you can go to church on your way back from breakfast? You just try it. You know you have to go across the compound to get to the chapel; you go without a guard, and I'm tellin' you those guards in the towers will cut you in half, Boy. You just forget it!" he snapped, as he turned away to lock the next prisoner in his cell.

I sat on my upper bunk and thought about it for some time. I was going to the Catholic service only because it was an excuse to get out of the cell for an hour. I sat in the back row with a few other guys, and used rubber bands to shoot paper clips at the priest's back.

"What do you want to go to church for, Ron?" Reuben asked. "There's no God anyway. It's all just a joke. If there were a God, He wouldn't have let my baby die in that fire. He wouldn't have scarred the other girl so bad. She's had to have twelve operations to try and fix her up. And all you have to do is to look around this place, and you know there's no God. Not a bit of human kindness in this hell hole."

I didn't answer Reuben because I had no answers. I was asking a lot of questions myself. If there's a God, why didn't He give me a daddy? If there's a God, why doesn't He take us out of this place? If there is a God, why doesn't He make somebody care about me?

The next morning I still had no answers to my questions, but I was going to see if those Adventists had any. Charlie seemed to think there was some good there, so I was going to cross that compound and see what would happen. If they cut me in half, then this miserable existence would be over. What was there to lose? From the breakfast line I could see that the notice was still on the bulletin board. I finished my breakfast in record time and was back in line to return to the cell. When the line started to move, I decided that when we came to the door leading out to the compound, I'd go through it. Fortunately, the guard was ahead of me and wasn't watching, so I eased through the door. Nonchalantly, I walked across the compound; not a shot was fired. Just inside the door on the other side was the chapel, and I walked right in and took a seat.

The service began with singing, and some of the songs I had heard before at the Lutheran church when I was a kid, so I sang along. Several guys nodded their heads in recognition that a new face had come to services, and at a break an older man came to greet me. "What's your name, Son?" he asked cordially. I answered him. "I'm glad you've come to join us. Are you an Adventist?"

"No, Sir. I'm nothing," I replied.

"Well, that doesn't matter. You're God's son, and that's what counts. Today we are having a special service, Son, and I wondered if you could help us out?" he asked.

"Sure, I'll help," I replied quickly, having no idea what he wanted me to do.

He went to the pulpit and opened the Bible. He read some verses, and then he talked about the night before Jesus was to be crucified. I'd heard about that before. He was saying how in the upper room Jesus washed the feet of the disciples before they ate the Last Supper. And then he said that Jesus had set an example for us that we should wash one another's feet also. He said something about humility. I thought, Oh no, they aren't going to make me . . .

Just about then, the man came back to me with a pan of water and a towel in his hands. He said. "I'll show you how we do it, Son." He knelt down in front of the prisoner next to me and put the pan of water on the floor at his feet. The guy took off his shoes and socks and put one foot in the basin. The man cupped his hand to gently pour water over the guy's foot. He held the foot in one hand then and washed with the other. Then he dried the foot and repeated the process with the other foot. When he was finished, the man stood to his feet and gave the prisoner a hug. "God Bless you, Boy," he said.

"God Bless you too, Brother Haswell."

Wow. These people are plum crazy, I thought. I would have run for my life if I could have, but I'd already promised to help. I washed the feet of a few guys, but I wouldn't let anyone touch mine.

I couldn't wait to get back to my cell! I must have washed my hands for ten minutes in the little stainless steel sink. I felt like gagging! For three days I was so sick to my stomach that I stayed in my cell rather than go to meals. I'm never going back to that church, I determined. They are a bunch of weirdos! Who ever heard of washing people's feet in church? What in the world was Charlie's problem?

By Wednesday I was feeling better. I was going to meals again, and I never said a word about my experience to Reuben. He was right. He had told me not to go, that there was no God, and he was right! There was no need to tell him so. I'd just forget the whole thing. So much for Charlie's big ideas! Instead of getting help from the Adventists, I got sick!

That following Friday our guard spoke to me as he let us out of the cell for chow. "I hope you don't think you're going to church tomorrow. I warned the tower guards, and they'll be watching for you. You step one foot on that compound without a guard escort, and they'll slice you in half!"

The funny thing was I had not planned on going to church until that very moment. He supplied me with a much-needed challenge, and I began to scheme about how I could get there just to bug him. Since I had no desire to wash feet again, there was nothing at that service of interest to me, so my desire to attend was purely one of spite. Until I fell asleep that night, I thought about how I could cross the compound. This time I wanted to survive. I couldn't let myself get shot!

After breakfast while returning to the cell, I broke line at the doorway to the compound just as I had done the previous week. I opened the door slowly, and before I made another move, I looked up at the three towers that I could see from the door. Sure enough, the guards in the towers all stood with their rifles pointed straight at me! I told myself, I've got a lot of guts, but I'm not stupid. I stood there for a while thinking. The guards can't pull a trigger until I walk out there alone, so I'll stay put. Soon I saw the garbage wagon on its way around the compound. A prisoner drove the two horses, and a guard with a rifle walked alongside the wagon. When they came close to where I was standing, I called to him and asked if he would escort me to the church.

"Come right along, Boy. I'll be happy to walk you to church." Wow! I hadn't heard a guard speak so politely since I'd been there. I cautiously walked out the door and right up to the guard, only two feet from me. We walked in silence, stopping twice more to pick up trash before we got to the other side of the compound and the safety of the church.

That same foot-washing man was there, and about thirty prisoners. They were choosing hymns to sing and asked if I had a favorite. Of course, I didn't, but I thumbed through the hymnal and found "What a Friend We Have in Jesus" and asked to add that one to the list. Brother Haswell came and sat beside me before the service started. He said he was so happy that I had come back and asked how long I had been in the "big house." We talked a few minutes, and finally I took the courage to tell him that the guard in my cellblock was giving me a hard time about coming to church. If nothing else, I thought perhaps I could get the guard in trouble. Leonard Haswell assured me that he would take care of it and that I wouldn't be bothered again.

During the service I watched and listened carefully to the lay preacher, not to what he was saying, particularly, but how he said it. I had to figure out what was so different about him, so intriguing. His manner was gentle, but there was no doubt that he was the one in charge. Nobody threw spitballs or paper clips at him. It seemed that all the guys who attended services admired and respected him greatly. You could tell that he had a genuine concern for the men, and they acted like they knew it.

The service was about to end, and Leonard Haswell was going to offer a closing prayer. I stood for a moment or two with my eyes open, watching him and trying to figure it out. Was it the way he was dressed? Was it his size? Was it the way he spoke? Was he like Charlie? He reminded me of someone I had seen or known before, but I couldn't put it together. But I did know one thing: I would come back again and again until I had figured it out! As long as they weren't washing feet again for a while, I would be back.

CHAPTER 10

Regardless of the reason I had sneaked to the Adventist services in the first place, after four or five weeks of regular attendance, I was hooked. It wasn't that the worship was much different from any other Protestant service or that the doctrines were so enticing. What attracted me there was Leonard Haswell, the lay pastor who came every Saturday morning from somewhere in Nashville to worship with "his boys," as he called us.

He spoke a lot about the love of a heavenly Father, but, to tell the truth, the word *father* made my skin crawl. The only father I had known was a man whose whole life modeled anger and cruelty. Every time the lay pastor said, "Father," referring, of course, to God, I would get a picture of mine. He was nothing at all like the "Father" that Leonard kept talking about.

My brother George had told me that his life of outright rebellion was a payback to the father who had beaten him unmercifully and had stripped him of any respect he might have had for Dad or his position in the family. He said that the final blow came to him on one of his birthdays, when he had been longing for a bicycle for some time. He had prayed for and dreamed of having a bike like his friends. The long-awaited birthday came, and George was excited and expectant. Dad called him out into the garage, and there in a crate was a bike. "Oh, is that for me, Dad?" little George asked.

"It **was** for you, but you've lost it because you screwed up yesterday. Now, it's going back to the store where I bought it," Dad said sarcastically. George said that he lost hope that day. All his hopes and dreams left him as surely as "his" bike had.

"I went nuts that day," George said. "What had happened wasn't fair, and Mother did nothing to stop the abuse or help me in any way. I made up my mind that I would get back at them. I would make them pay for what they had done to me, what Dad had done." George had made them pay, but he paid an even bigger price for his revenge.

I had so many questions about my father: *How could he have been so cruel to his own flesh and blood? What had happened to him as a boy to make him so filled with anger that everyone "walked on eggshells" around him? Didn't his conscience ever hurt him when he was going to sleep at night and thinking about all that had happened in the day? Didn't he ever feel bad for the things he said and did?* I remember asking him why he beat George and never touched me—not to spank or beat me and not to hold and love me either. Dad said that he tried to beat good sense into George, but it didn't work. So he took the opposite tactic with me. But his indifference didn't work either. I would rather have taken the beatings than be at the other end of his coldness, his distance.

I kept attending the Adventist services, and the hymns we sang over and over gradually began to mean something to me.

> Some glad mornin' when this life is o'er,
> I'll fly away.
> To a home on God's celestial shore,
> I'll fly away.
> I'll fly away, oh glory. I'll fly away.
> When I die, hallelujah bye and bye,
> I'll fly away.

"I'll Fly Away" was a favorite of the prisoners. Even a quick scan of the words makes that understandable. I wished that I could fly away, too, but eventual escape to heaven seemed no more likely to me than a fairytale's coming true. I had to see some tangible evidence that God cared for me if I was going to believe. The possibility of another world—either good or bad—was scary, too, because I'd promised God that I would take my dad's place in hell. At sixteen I concluded that my father belonged in hell. But I longed so intensely to have his approval and a relationship with him that I was willing to burn, if that's what happened to you in hell, in order to relate to Dad some way.

Some guy would always request that we sing "Amazing Grace." I would sing the words, but they did not ring true to my current experience. The line, "That saved a wretch like me," is a good example. I was a wretch all right, but compared to some of the guys in that prison, I thought I wasn't so bad. "I once was lost, but now I'm found. I was blind, but now I see." I took those lines literally. I remember thinking that I was never lost; I always knew how to get where I was going. And I was never blind either. These songs, I would think, are really stupid. What makes these guys cry when they sing them, and where does their enthusiasm for singing come from? Is religion some kind of scam? Have all these guys been fooled?

Once I was settled into the prison and its ways, I was assigned to the Classification Center using skills I had learned at El Reno. My days were filled with work, and my evenings were filled with Bible study. Pastors from several other denominations were "courting me," trying to interest me in their churches too. But I wasn't ready for a church. I didn't even know God yet, and I wasn't sure the Bible was true; so I had some investigating to do. I was taking two correspondence courses from the Adventists. Leonard had helped me sign up for these courses, thinking it would help answer some of my questions and would help me occupy my time. One was from an organization that had a radio program called *The Voice of Prophecy.* The other course was from an organization that produced the television broadcast called *Faith For Today.* Both lessons started out with the fundamentals, and that was great since I knew almost nothing of the Bible. Fortunately, by that time Bibles were again available to prisoners who requested them.

I had made some good friends in the Classification Center as well as at the church. One day at work I was offered a small radio with an earplug. It ran by battery, but the battery was missing. I could have it for ten dollars if I wanted it. Now the interesting part is that radios were contraband for prisoners, but I had a perfect place to hide it—behind a brick in the wall of the photo lab where I also worked. My pay as a prisoner then was one dollar per month, and that was made available to buy stamps or candy bars. I chose to buy the little radio and paid for it at one dollar a month for ten months.

The corrected Bible lessons that were returned to me were a welcome oasis in the dessert of prison because each one contained a little note of encouragement and uplift; and as time progressed, the notes became more personal. I found it difficult to wade through the material and compare notes in an attempt to discover real truth. At one point the issue of the Sabbath was presented by both of the Adventist courses. There were so many texts proving the validity of the Sabbath that it was hard to ignore. I'd always been the kind of kid who wanted the real truth even though I often didn't tell it. The facts were important to me, and Leonard and a fellow prisoner, Lonnie, presented them in a clear and sensible manner. On the other hand, pastors from other churches were doing the same, and, in addition, were offering me scholarships to attend their colleges after my release. I guess I was being bribed.

One evening I went to the darkroom and took my radio from its hiding place, ready for some recreation. I had obtained a battery from a prison employee who had taken a liking to me. I took the radio with me, hidden in the small of my back, to the restroom. There I sat on the only seat in that little room with the earplug in my ear and the radio hidden under my shirt. As I turned the dial looking for some music, I heard men's voices singing a familiar song, one that we had sung in Leonard's service. "Lift up the trumpet and loud let it ring. Jesus is coming again." I carefully adjusted the dial to get the clearest reception possible.

The singing stopped and a man's voice—a very kind voice—began to speak. I heard him say that the program was called *The Voice of Prophecy.* H.M.S. Richards was speaking that evening about the Sabbath, the first in a series on that topic that would run for several weeks. For the next half hour, I was glued to the earphone and the message that came through it. Presenting clearly and softly, Pastor Richards spoke of the first Sabbath in the Garden of Eden. He read from the Bible that on the seventh day God had rested from all the work He had done. I started counting: Monday, Tuesday, Wednesday . . . something was wrong. It wasn't coming out right. According to my figuring, Sunday was day seven.

After the broadcast was over, I left the restroom, replaced the radio in its hiding place, and went to the Classification Center to look at a calendar. Wait! The first day of the week was Sunday, not Monday. I counted on my fingers: Sunday, Monday, Tuesday.... Yes! Saturday **was** the seventh day. Whew! Well, that settles that, I thought, as I walked back to my cell.

I was now an honor prisoner and had the privilege of walking inside the prison walls, in the Classification Center only, without a guard at my side. When I returned to the cell, Reuben asked where I had been. "Just in the photo lab," I replied, knowing that I had told only part of the truth. I couldn't tell him about the radio and what I had heard, not yet anyway. I fell asleep that night comforted that I had heard the truth. I was elated!

During the week before the next Sabbath, however, the prison chaplain and the Pentecostal preacher talked to me about Sunday being the Lord's Day. They told me that the Sabbath had been done away with at the Crucifixion. I was confused again! I went to Leonard with my questions when Saturday services rolled around. He put his arm on my shoulder and said that my faith was being tested and that he would keep me in his prayers during the week. "Study, Son, just keep studying, and the Lord will show you the truth," he said. Then he actually gave me a little hug, and I melted from his tenderness. This man was a true father-type, I thought.

What? A father? I looked at him again as he spoke to another guy. That was it! He reminded me of my father. I thought to myself, he's nothing like your father! But he was! He was not as tall as Stanley Rockey, but Leonard Haswell looked enough like my father to be a brother! It took my breath away. So that's why I have been so fascinated by him, so impressed with his knowledge and his gentle, but firm, treatment of the prisoners. This was my father, not in behavior, but in appearance. This is what I had longed for all of my life—a father, and here was one who wanted to relate to me, who called me "son," who was interested in my thoughts, my needs, my questions. He touched me, hugged me. He came to me rather than my always wanting to go to him. What a switch! And right there, at that moment, I felt at home.

There, inside the prison walls of the toughest prison in the country outside of Alcatraz, I felt the security of home. It was a while before I would understand that it wasn't just Leonard's appearance, the fact that he looked so much like my own father, that made me feel so at home. That lesson I would learn later.

Eventually I was convinced that Saturday was the Sabbath, and I had made up my mind to observe it the way that the fourth commandment teaches. But I now had a new problem. All prisoners were required to attend the movies on Saturday afternoons, and, to me, attending them would not be observing the Sabbath hours in a way that would honor God. I was not accustomed to praying about problems, but I decided to see whether God would help me in this situation. "God, what do You want me to do about this business of movies on the Sabbath? You'll have to show me somehow," I prayed.

That afternoon the guards came to get us for the movies. Obediently I got in line, and, walking to the theater, I prayed again. "I guess I have to go today, God, but could You make this movie a blessing to me, please?"

The movie shown that day was *The Days of Wine and Roses.* I had no idea what the film was about, but settled into my seat expecting a blessing. And that's just what I got! The story was of a married couple who were both alcoholics. The movie illustrated the devastation caused when alcohol is a partner in a marriage and family. I was an alcoholic, and I needed that message. Yes, I was in prison where alcohol was not available, but I longed for the day I would be released so that I could slip, once again, into the familiar numbness that I thought kept me sane. The point of the film that most impressed me was that alcohol had divided a husband and wife who had loved each other dearly when they married. The movie ends with the wife abandoning her husband and replacing him with the bottle.

I lay on my bunk for a long time that night, trying to fall asleep. I thought of my mother and the closeness I did not have with her. I thought of Phyllis, my other mother, and felt a twinge of loneliness for her. I thought of Joan and of her parents. They were the couple in the movie, estranged by the bottle—or perhaps they used the bottle to numb the pain of their estrangement. And then I wondered what would it have been like for Joan and me if we had stayed together.

In the breakfast line the following Friday, I saw a new notice on the bulletin board. It stated that movies would now be shown on Saturday mornings instead of Saturday afternoons. The other Adventist prisoners and I could go to church while the rest of the guys went to the show. God had answered my prayer twice. First with the movie that made plain to me the devastation that alcohol can bring to a marriage and then with the schedule changes that facilitated Sabbath keeping. But it was still difficult for me to believe that God cared about me enough to answer my prayer. No, I decided, it must be just a coincidence.

As the weeks passed by, I learned much more from the Adventists than just the Sabbath truth. One thing I learned was what the Bible says about unclean foods. Now that was going to create a real problem for me because much of the prison food was cooked in lard. I accepted this new challenge eagerly. I would see which of the guys would barter with me. I'd give them my pork for their bread or vegetables. That worked fairly well. Then I would spend my dollar a month on peanuts for protein. Even though my diet wasn't the best, I began to feel better without all the grease.

When I had entered the federal prison in El Reno, I was frightened because I had seen in Shelby County Jail what happened to the skinny kids. I decided that I needed to add weight and power, and the facilities were available there to do so. Every day I ate a pint of ice cream and worked out on weights. One day a fellow prisoner punched me, and I was shocked by what happened when I retaliated by punching back. It felt like I had a locomotive engine behind my fist instead of a toy wagon. After that, the sex-hungry prisoners left me alone. I was willing to leave the results of my diet in God's hands. I figured that if he could take care of Daniel and his friends in the biblical account, I would try to trust Him to do the same for me.

Every Sunday evening I went to the darkroom at the same time. Of course, I occasionally would go there during the week to work, so I hoped that the guards wouldn't suspect something strange. Eventually they did ask why I was always missing about the same time in the evening, but I was able to convince them that darkroom responsibilities kept me going there regularly. After that encounter, I was careful to vary my times in the darkroom as much as possible. I didn't want to miss my Sunday-night date with H.M.S. Richards and the quartet, and I also didn't want to get caught. That would forfeit my honor status and the radio broadcast I so enjoyed.

Even though I was learning a lot from attending the Adventist services and studying the Bible correspondence courses, I still knew very little about what God is really like or what it means to follow Him. I was ambivalent about the submitting to a heavenly Father. My relationship with my earthly father made me afraid of my heavenly Father. How could I possibly give my life to a Father I couldn't even see, a Father I couldn't believe cared about me or would listen to me? At the same time, I was attracted to the idea of a loving heavenly Father, the kind of God Leonard talk about. I finally decided that if Leonard was right, God would just have to prove to me somehow that He cared about me.

CHAPTER 11

Lonnie Melton and I had become quite good chums for prison comrades. We had the church in common, and Lonnie, very knowledgeable about the Bible, had taken me under his wing and studied more difficult teachings with me. There were other prisoners also who had been studying for some time and were also helpful to my information-gathering and decision-making process. Of course, the only time that we could confer was during the two hours we were allowed to be at the services on Saturday mornings.

During the week, other chaplains or pastors who came from the outside endeavored to convince me of the particular teachings they believed, and then in church I would run that information by Leonard Haswell and Lonnie; and they would point out scripture that either supported or refuted the teaching.

I was particularly fascinated by some of the metaphysical teachings of the Unity Church, such as their belief that the mind controls the body, that we are who we think we are, and that positive thinking inevitably produces positive behaviors. Those ideas seemed to ring true to me; they made sense. Because of it, I was being strongly influenced to be a part of their denomination. I'll have to admit, too, that the free college tuition that they offered me was powerfully influencing my decision making.

One week at the Saturday church service, I had the opportunity to spend some time alone with Leonard. He was kind and gentle with me and so understanding of the dilemma I was facing. When I explained the particular Unity belief that was drawing me to their denomination, he said, "Well, Son, next week I'll bring you something to read that I think you will find most interesting. It's a book entitled *The Ministry of Healing,* and I believe that you will find information in that book similar to what you've been telling me. You're not really in a rush to make a decision, so why don't you wait until I come back next week with that book? Read it and then tell me what you think. How does that sound?"

I think that I would have agreed with almost anything that Leonard requested me to do because of the manner in which he treated me. The fatherly way he listened and counseled felt so good to my needy heart.

True to his word, Leonard brought the book to church the following week, and I read it ravenously. I was excited. It was written in such an understandable way and made so much good sense. Amazingly, I had never before—in school or outside of school—read a book all the way through. I had hated reading and seldom ever picked up a book unless it was pornographic or contained a lot of pictures. And now here in prison I was becoming an avid reader.

I continued to work at the Classification Center of the prison and also continued my Sunday-night visits to the darkroom, where I could take out that little hidden radio and listen to my favorite program. The speaker, a man whom I had never met, became closer to me than any family member. His voice was soothing and kind, and, regardless what topic he was presenting, I felt a fatherly presence as I listened. He would always end the program with a four-line poem that began with "Have faith in God." His words were encouraging, and his manner soothing and comforting to me.

Occasionally on Saturdays other men, some of them ministers, would come with Leonard to the services. Kenneth Holland, then an editor at Southern Publishing Association, was one of those visitors. They did their best to become acquainted with the prisoners individually, and several were hired at the press after they were released from prison.

Prison life, regardless of the wonderful things I was learning there, was not easy for me. Even though I liked to be alone and I had loved to hide in confined spaces as a child, forced confinement was traumatic. I had been given "wings" as a very young child; seldom did I have to account for my whereabouts or even the time that I came home at night. I recall being five and six years of age and having the freedom to roam the town with my friend Tommy and never being required to "report in." As a prisoner, there are no private places, no wings, and no freedom. My only consolation was that I had discovered my escape route and knew that if it ever got so rough that I couldn't bear it, I could always do as I had done at Shelby County. The biggest deterrent from running was the fear that I would be caught again and have to pay the price of more prison time for a second escape.

About eight or nine months after arriving at Nashville State Penitentiary, I had heard that Leonard, who had some kind of political pull with the Commissioner of Corrections, could petition for a prisoner to get out early if he thought that the prisoner was converted. While I really loved Leonard and appreciated the loving concern he had for the others and me, I was willing to use him just to get out. At that time I had no idea where I'd go once I got out because I really had no home. Of course, Johnny and Phyllis would be kind to me, but I felt it wasn't appropriate for me to go there and stay. Anyway, I wanted to be footloose and fancy free and not in any way tied to my mother. I feared that if I went back to Milwaukee where the family was, they'd expect all kinds of stuff from me, and really I had nothing to offer. Regardless of having nowhere to go, I wanted out!

I remember asking Lonnie, "Well, how do converted people act? How can anybody else tell if you're converted or not?" I thought that if I knew the behaviors and I put them on like a coat, maybe Leonard would notice and think about talking to the Commissioner in my behalf.

According to Lonnie, one of the outward signs of the inward change was to be publicly baptized. My family had told me that I'd been baptized in the Lutheran church as a baby, and I wondered what would happen if I were baptized again. But my desire to get out of the Nashville prison was so great that I was willing to take the risk. Lonnie told me that a baptism was coming up in a couple of weeks, so I decided to take the plunge, and, for Adventists, the plunge is literal. They believe in baptism by immersion, and at the penitentiary, that was going to be an unusual experience.

You can be certain that Nashville State Penitentiary did not have something as luxurious as a swimming pool, and there were no provisions for temporary leave, even to go to a church for baptism. In the past, they had made do with whatever they could find in which a body could be totally immersed. By the time of my baptism, however, the new church had a baptistry. Leonard had told me that baptism was a symbolic burial. All my sins would stay in the bottom of the tank, and I was to be resurrected into a new life. As I understood it, when I would come up out of the water, everything would be new and different for me. It was as if my mind was to be washed with a powerful detergent, and it would be totally impossible for it to get dirty again. Wouldn't that be great? But I still faced the dilemma about my bargain with God about my dad.

The day of the baptism my thinking was just as confused as it had been for some time. I knew that the Adventists were sincere, and I sincerely wanted to be different—but I doubted there was even a ghost of a chance that I could change. How does a guy who has made a deal with God to be more like the devil, take the risk of having his mind cleansed? Would the contract with God be null and void once I was baptized? I just didn't want to take the risk of my dad having to go to eternal death just because I screwed up again! There was a war between satisfying my own needs and keeping my promise for my dad's sake. As usual, I chose the self-centered option. I had to get out of that prison if at all possible.

I was disappointed to learn that an ordained pastor had to perform the baptism. I would have preferred Leonard to baptize me because I could trust him. A Pastor N. C. Johnson came to the prison with Leonard for the occasion. Leonard was so happy that day, actually triumphant. I was happy too—happy to be making Leonard happy. A beautiful black leather Bible was given to me by some caring people from the outside. This Bible became my treasure and a symbol of that event. I was emotionally high for a few days because I had pleased my dad, not my blood father but my spiritual father.

The only difference I felt when I came up out of that water is that I was wet. It wasn't a real disappointment to me, however, because I somehow knew before the event that I wouldn't be that much different after it. So I played the game of making myself look good for several weeks, and, little by little I did notice some slight changes in my thinking.

Leonard Haswell had been coming week after week to the prison for a long time, and, because of his work, an actual church was organized inside the walls. There were elders, deacons, and other elected or appointed officers. Since I was very actively involved in the church, I was asked to be an elder. Unfortunately, I did not fully understand the responsibilities of an elder, nor was I really prepared. I just knew that elders were to speak from time to time, conduct song service, and occasionally visit other prisoners who were sick enough to be in the prison infirmary. So one Saturday when an ordained pastor came to the prison with Leonard, I was ordained.

In order to visit the infirmary, we had to be escorted by a prison guard. Sometimes Leonard would accompany us; other times just one or two of the ordained prisoner elders would go alone. On one such Saturday, I went to visit the sick; one of the patients was an elderly prisoner who had been incarcerated for many years. He was dying of cancer and was in excruciating pain from being unable to urinate for three days. Beads of perspiration poured from his face, and he moaned and groaned in agony. I am not sure whether the attendants were giving him medication to relieve his pain, but it was heart wrenching to see him suffering so.

He asked me to read to him from the Psalms, and for about twenty minutes I did so. I had not learned to read well and certainly was not used to reading aloud, but I managed rather well. Then he asked if I would pray for him. I knelt there beside his bed and hardly knew what to say, but I do remember asking God to somehow relieve this extreme pain he was in by allowing him to urinate. I held his hand and could feel his hand trembling in mine. I remember feeling so helpless and wishing that this sweet old man could have a sense of peace while he was dying. It must be bad enough to be dying, but having to die in prison, alone, was hard for me to see.

As soon as I got to my feet after the prayer, he said, "Young man, could you be kind enough to pass me that urinal?" As I did, I offered up another silent plea, "Please, God . . ." In seconds, that man was urinating.

This experience was impossible to ignore or to dismiss as just a coincidence. I played with it for a long time in my mind and was still thinking about it as I went to sleep that night. Had God really answered **my** prayer? Had He used **me** to be a blessing to that old prisoner? Was something really strange happening to me? Had I really been converted, after all?

One Saturday after services several weeks later, Leonard talked to me privately.

"I've got an appointment for you a week from Monday with the Commissioner of Corrections, Ron. If that appointment goes well, if you are able to impress him with your behavior and with the good record you have since you've been here, there's an excellent chance that you can get out of prison early," he said confidentially.

To say that I was thrilled would be stating it mildly! I floated back to my cell and could hardly wait to tell Reuben about it. Reuben seemed to be happy for me. He had seen me devouring reading materials and writing out the Bible correspondence lessons, but, as far as I could tell, he was still guarded about the value of religion. "Be careful, Ron," he cautioned. "I've been here almost ten years, and I've seen a lot of guys get out 'cause they got religion. But religion doesn't keep them out. Lots of them end right back here where they got their religion."

That night I spent a long time thinking and then praying about what Reuben had said. As a matter of fact, I could hardly sleep for the next week. Over and over in my head came the questions about conversion. Was I really converted? Or was I just thinking and behaving like I was so that I could get out early? Seemingly out of nowhere had come a conscience that I hadn't felt for years, a little voice in my head that I hadn't heard in a long, long time. I began to worry about how all this would affect Leonard if I should end up back in the penitentiary after he had helped me to get an early release. I wondered how many of "his boys" that had happened to. It seemed to me that this man was so dedicated to us cons that to disappoint him would be a crime. I remembered one week when his wife had had a heart attack; he actually left her hospital bed to come to the prison so as to not disappoint us. How could I hurt him?

That was one of the hardest weeks in my prison term there. Night after night I tossed and turned in my bunk, greatly troubled. How would I know for sure? What should I do? I prayed and prayed but wasn't sure what to pray for. I had promised God that I would never bother Him again if He would just take my dad to heaven, and here I was bothering Him! And the hard part was that I didn't really know what to ask for! Perhaps just the relief of a clean conscience. "Please, please, God!" I begged. But would He hear, would He care to hear, considering the bargain?

Saturday morning finally arrived, and I was up, washed, and ready to get in the chow line early. During the previous night, I had finally decided what I was going to do, and I was anxious to get it over with. Breakfast dragged on and on, and the usual fifteen-minute race through the meal felt like fifteen hours. I had to get to Leonard; I had to tell him what I'd decided!

Once seated in the pew, I kept turning around looking for Leonard to arrive. What would I do if he didn't show up? Lonnie went to the pulpit and started a song service. I wanted to sing, but I was preoccupied with the need to talk to Leonard. We sang "A Wonderful Savior Is Jesus, My Lord," "Precious Memories," and then "I'll Fly Away." Just as we were starting "In the Garden," Leonard walked in. That I didn't just jump up out of my seat and grab him is surprising indeed, considering my anxiety. I wanted to, but, since he was late, I would have to wait until services were over.

"Good morning, Men," he said, and went immediately into his message for the day. My head was elsewhere! There was no way I could concentrate on the sermon. I just wanted it to be over so I could talk to Leonard. He asked me to have the main prayer for the service, and I did, but I was so preoccupied with my agenda that I have no idea what I prayed about.

At the close of the service, I approached Leonard and begged for a few minutes to talk with him privately. "Brother Haswell," I said.

"Yes, Son, what is it? You seem upset about something. What's wrong?"

"Well, Sir, I've decided that I don't want to keep that appointment with the Commissioner on Monday," I said sheepishly.

"What, Boy? You have a good chance to get out early, probably a better chance than anyone else here I know. What's this about, Son?"

"I believe you, but I just have to be sure. I've decided that I want to serve all of the time that I owe the state of Tennessee. Would that be OK?" I asked.

Tears swelled in Leonard's eyes, and he threw his arms around me. "I do understand, Son, and I'm proud, very proud of you. God bless you, Boy." Leonard and I both sniffled a bit, and when our eyes met, we really saw each other. There was an understanding between us that I had never experienced with any other man. How is it that someone, not your own, can so thoroughly understand you? I wondered.

Back in the cell, I chose to not speak to Reuben of my decision. I would just keep this one to myself. But now I had some other work to do with God. "How am I going to know, how will I be able to tell if You and I really have something going, God? There's got to be a way that You can get this across to me. I have no clue as to what to tell You what I would need in order to know for sure. But You know, and I'll leave it to You. And then when, or if, something does happen, I'll just know that it's You telling me that we're OK."

CHAPTER 12

When my release date drew near, I wrote to my mother and asked her to look in the phone book for the name of a Seventh-day Adventist minister living in Milwaukee. In a return letter she said that there were several listed, and she had chosen one from the list and sent his name and address to me.

In preparation for my release, I wrote to Pastor Joseph S. Damazo of the Milwaukee Central Church. I was looking for a pastor who would take some interest in me because when I got out on my own, I would have no spiritual support and guidance. Almost immediately, he began to correspond with me. He provided information about the three churches then in the city and assured me that he would be looking forward to my arrival. I sensed in his letters a genuine welcoming spirit and a true desire to be a mentor and guide and to become acquainted with my family already living in the Milwaukee area.

While a prisoner in Nashville, I actually completed seventeen Bible courses. For many of them I received certificates, which were special to me because I had no high-school diploma. Week after week I had the privilege of leading out in the prison services. We had a church choir and some fine religious music in our services. One of the gospel songs that became a favorite, one that we sang frequently was "There's Room at the Cross for You." Perhaps the words were especially significant to me because all my life I had needed a secure place to hide. The Cross was becoming for me a true shelter in which I could hide.

During his thirty-day induction period in the Classification Center, I met a new prisoner about my age with a life sentence ahead of him.

We talked several times about what he was facing, and I began to share with him what I had found behind the frightening walls. I began studying the Bible with Ellis, brought him to church with me, and introduced him to Leonard and Lonnie. Before I was released, I saw him baptized. What a thrill it was to see some hope begin to appear in the eyes of a very discouraged young man. It felt so rewarding to have had a part in introducing him to a new source of strength and comfort for the long years he was facing. I began to wonder if once I was out of prison, I could prepare myself to become a minister. "What will You have me to do, God?" became a regular prayer.

It would be very difficult for me to leave Leonard Haswell. He had truly become a father, the kind I had longed for all my life. Now I would have to rely on Pastor Damazo to take up the job of spiritual mentoring. I knew that my brother-in-law, Johnny, would still welcome me and be as merciful to me as he always had been, but I would need someone who believed as I did, and to whom a spiritual life was important, to guide me in the first few months out of the "big house."

At last my release date was announced. Reuben and I had become dear friends, but he wasn't ready or willing to hear about the new faith that I had found. Admittedly, I had my ups and downs and times when I doubted, but they were brief. I now seldom thought of the contract I had made years before with God to go to hell so that my father could go to heaven. I realized now that we could both be in heaven together, that God would not hold me to such a bargain—especially since He hadn't asked me to make it in the first place. I was beginning to comprehend some of the love that God has for His children, even though I had not seen it demonstrated by my own father in my most important character-forming years.

Finally, the day of my release from the penitentiary arrived. It was a Saturday, but I was allowed to go to church services before leaving. On that day, Ellis and I sang a duet we had prepared, and we dedicated it to Leonard. We had practiced the song and knew it well. After we sang, we told Leonard that this song, "Anywhere With Jesus," was supposed to be a favorite of Adventists. At that one moment, he hurt and embarrassed me, unintentionally, I'm sure. He took the wind right out of my sails by telling me that he'd never heard the hymn before! I was devastated, but it was perhaps ordained. Almost immediately I recalled a text I had memorized about not putting your trust in man or making flesh your arm. Up until that moment, Leonard had never disappointed me. I believe that through this insignificant incident, though not so insignificant at the time, that God was encouraging me to rely solely on Him. This was part of the preparation for life outside the prison walls.

I had been invited to prepare and preach the sermon for that last day I was incarcerated. Forty or fifty men, all dressed the same, all emotionally and spiritually free behind the walls of the most feared prison in the South, sat in my congregation. It was a tearful service for me because, for the first time in my life, I had come become emotionally close to people. I had a father, Leonard; I had brothers, Lonnie and the other guys who regularly attended church; and I had found a safe hiding place. No longer did I have to hide under a bridge or a dining-room table, but in my mind there was a safe place, a home, the presence of the Father.

I remember going back to my cell, where I was to take off the prison attire and change into civilian clothes. They had chosen a gray pinstripe suit, a white shirt, and a thin black tie. I would walk out of prison looking as ordinary as any guy outside the walls. Reuben was there, and he watched as I took off the familiar and put on the strange. I gathered together the few things that were mine: my precious black leather Bible, my certificates, and the religious books I had collected and read.

Finally Reuben spoke. "Ron," he said, "I have seen some wonderful changes in you since you've been here. When you came, you had the foulest mouth I had ever heard! You were angry and arrogant, and that has softened. You have read and studied, and you have been regular at church attendance. I really hope that you will make it on the outside. I hope I never see you back in this place again."

I shook his hand, and then, on impulse, I hugged him. He had been a wonderful model and comforting friend, and I would miss him. I grabbed the box that contained my treasures and called for the guard to let me out. I was ready to face the world, to get on a bus, and travel to Milwaukee, to meet my new mentor. I had no clue how, but, having seen the way that God provided in Nashville, surely He would continue on the outside!

"Ron, do you think that I could have just one of your books?" Reuben asked. I stopped short in my tracks.

"No, Reuben, you can't," I said. "You can have them all, except for my Bible, that is. I can get new books out there." As I placed the box on the bunk beside him, I noticed that his eyes had filled with tears.

"I'll believe, Ron, when I see your name on a sign outside of a church—'Ron Rockey, Pastor.' Yeah, then I'll believe that there's a God."

I patted his shoulder and walked out the door. I heard it clang behind me, and, looking back, I saw Reuben, head in his hands, alone again.

"Well, Rockey, you got religion in here. Well, I'll tell you. I've seen a lot of guys come in here and get religion and, because of it, get out early, like you. And in no time at all, they end up right back here, where they started. That's how much good that religion did for them. So we'll see how long it takes for you to come back," the old guard growled.

"Well, Sir," I responded, "I've served every day that I owe the state of Tennessee, and I figure it this way: If I go out these doors with religion and I come right back in here, I haven't lost a thing. But if I go out with religion and I stay out, I've gained everything."

As we approached the last door, the passage to freedom, the guard handed me an envelope. "Here's your release papers and enough cash to get you home," he said, patting my arm. "Good luck, Rockey!"

I walked out that last door like I was walking on air, hardly daring to believe that I was really finally out, free at last. The cement walkway from the front door of the stone castlelike building to the last guardhouse is very long, too long. Somehow, I suspected that when I left Tennessee's penitentiary, I wouldn't be as free as I wanted to be, and as I walked the long walk, I was praying that my hunches had been wrong. As I approached the last guardhouse, I noticed a man dressed in a business suit, and, for a second, I felt a lurch in the pit of my stomach. Maybe just a visitor coming in, I thought. I got as far as the guardhouse when the stranger approached. "Are you Ronald Rockey?" he asked.

"Yes, Sir," I replied. There was that stomach feeling again, jumping up to my throat.

"I have a retainer from the state of Wisconsin to take you back to face charges against you there." I said nothing, but my heart sank. He took my Bible and the envelope from me, pulled the handcuffs from his belt and pulled my arms behind me, locking those feared stainless-steel bands around my wrists. He carried my Bible and the statement of release to a police car awaiting us in the parking lot. Local Nashville police had obviously brought him to pick me up. They pushed me into the back seat of the car, and then the Wisconsin detective told me that I had a choice. We would go to a bus station for a bus ride back to Wisconsin or to the airport for a flight. The choice was mine. He explained to me that in order to fly, he would have to remove my handcuffs on the plane.

"That'll be fine with me if we fly, but if you make one false move," he said, "you'll be back in handcuffs in a breath, and we'll be taking the bus!"

I told him that I understood and was determined to prove that I wasn't going anywhere but back to Milwaukee. The prospect of being cuff-free was far more appealing than a long bus ride in handcuffs. I'd be sure to have a horrific headache if I had to be in those cuffs for a long time.

In a short time we were at the Nashville Airport and boarding a plane to Chicago. As soon as I got on the plane and needed to fasten the seat belt, the awful handcuffs were removed. The detective was friendly as soon as we were away from the other policemen, and on the plane we talked a lot. He was interested in my plans for the future and also questioned me extensively about the conditions at the Nashville Penitentiary. He told me that I would be taken to the Milwaukee County Jail to await trial. Actually, the flight was enjoyable, and considering that I wasn't bound in cuffs, I did feel that I was at least tasting freedom.

We landed at Chicago's O'Hare Airport, then the busiest airport in the world. The remainder of the trip would be by car, so we walked out into the terminal to get to the appointed car. Suddenly I noticed that the detective was not beside me. I panicked! God help me, I thought, as I stopped dead in my tracks. The thought came to me that I shouldn't move. So there I stood with people having to walk around me. I looked in every direction, but there was no sight of the detective.

"If he's just hiding where he can see me and waiting to see what I'll do, I won't move. That way he can't think that I'm trying to ditch him. If we truly have lost each other somehow, I'll let him find me. When he does, he'll know that I wasn't trying to run. I'm out here in the middle of the crowd, people walking all around and bumping into me, but I'm not moving!" I decided.

I stood there in one spot for fifteen or twenty minutes. I remember thinking that I'd stay there until midnight, or at least until someone came and asked me why I was standing there motionless. If I am asked, I can always ask them to page the detective, I thought. I was determined that there would be no excuse to slap me in handcuffs or to "get me" for attempted escape.

"There you are, Rockey," I heard someone say. The detective was standing beside me.

"Yes, Sir. About fifteen minutes ago I noticed that you weren't walking beside me, and I immediately stopped dead still. I figured that you would find me if you were the only one moving," I answered. Not another word was spoken about the test he gave me, but I knew that very moment that he'd been watching me all the time. This had been a test, and apparently I'd passed!

CHAPTER 13

My hometown welcomed me with open arms, ushered me straight through an open cell door, and locked it behind me. It had been a strenuous few hours on the journey from Nashville Penitentiary to Milwaukee County Jail, and I was exhausted and disheartened. I had been set free only to be imprisoned again. I sat on the cot in yet another set of prison attire, with my head in my hands, crying out to God."Why am I here? What are You doing to me?"

I tried to remember what I had done to have caused this detour, what old debt the state of Wisconsin was trying to collect. I remembered stealing money from several places but had difficulty remembering exactly which offenses I had committed before serving in the navy and which ones afterward. Finally, I fell into a troubled sleep, tossing and turning most of the night, alternating between sleeping and praying.

I expected to learn on Monday morning just when my court date would be. That would mean languishing another twenty-four hours in jail with my inebriated and drug-addicted fellow prisoners. I spent Sunday reading the only thing I had, my Bible, and praying that Sunday night would be my last behind bars.

On Monday morning the jail officers approached me. I was told that my bail had been set at two hundred and fifty dollars, and I was given the opportunity to make a phone call. I phoned the home of Phyllis and Johnny, where my birth mother still lived. I told them that I had been returned to Milwaukee and was in the local jail until bail could be arranged or a court appearance met. Of course, I hoped that it would be possible for them to find the bail money from somewhere. Surely, if everyone contributed, they could come up with that small amount, I thought. I asked my mother to call Pastor Damazo to let him know my situation and location. Then I waited anxiously for the bail to be paid, the cell door to be opened, and my family to stand on the other side, awaiting my release.

Pastor Damazo was my first visitor. He was ushered into my cell after having been introduced to me by a guard. Within moments I felt that I had found a comrade. He spent quite a bit of time with me that first visit, and we talked about my past and about the local church. We prayed together that my release would be soon, and we asked God to guide my plans for the future.

As the days rolled into weeks, my doubts about God's leading sapped my energy and enthusiasm, and my discouragement grew. Why would it be God's will for me to spend time in yet another prison? Couldn't He find greater things for me to do outside than inside Wisconsin's walls? How could I prepare for ministry and be inside a prison? It just didn't make any sense that Milwaukee was keeping me inside its jail when I could be outside, beginning to make restitution for the money I had taken.

Pastor Damazo and his associate, Pastor Skilton, visited me faithfully. On one of Pastor Skilton's visits, he brought with him a little paperback book entitled *Steps to Christ,* and he suggested that I read it carefully. He also gave me a two-colored pencil. On one end was blue lead and on the other, red.

"This is what I want you to do, Son," he said. "Underline everything that's important in blue pencil and everything that's super important, everything that speaks to you personally, in red. Read and reread this book until it becomes a part of you. I believe that it will help you through this tough period of waiting. And just know, Son, that we are super-anxious for you to come out of this place. We are anxious to have you as an important part of our church family and to help prepare you for service for the Lord." He prayed with me before he left the cell, this time with his hand on my shoulder.

After he left, I plunked myself down on my cot with the little book still in my hand. I had to process some emotions before I could read. There was that word again—*son.* Leonard had said it, and now the pastor here said it too. Why was it that when someone called me "son," it softened me every time? I knew that I am God's son, at least that's what I had been told. Somehow, when Leonard called me "son," it meant so much more. And now this pastor called me "son." Maybe the impact was so strong because I was never really anybody's son until I met Leonard. I really missed him.

I fanned through the pages and glanced at the chapter titles. I didn't feel like reading but forced myself to read for a while since reading was the only thing to keep me from pacing. I found myself doing some underlining in blue and, now and again, a few red lines. But persistent thoughts and fears haunted me, interrupting my reading: Did my family really want me to be still locked up in this place? Had they honestly tried to obtain bail, or were they lying to me when they said that they couldn't raise the money? Was I now, and had I always been so incorrigible that no one out there wanted me? I remembered the time my brother George told Dad that if the family really wanted to get rid of him, Dad should sign papers giving George permission to go into the armed services. Dad had willingly signed, lying about George's age, just to get rid of his own son. Sure, George was a problem, but that was because Dad had beaten him all the time. Sure, I was a problem, but had I created so much hell for the family that, just like George, they didn't want me, either?

Pastor Damazo seemed to want me to be on the outside. He and Pastor Skilton were so faithful in visiting me that they seemed more like family to me than my very own, but I even questioned why they didn't help to get me out on bail. What was God doing? Why wasn't He answering my prayers the way He had when I was in Nashville? Had I done something to slip from His grace? I thought and thought about nothing else until I thought I'd loose my mind.

Three months had gone by. Summer had turned to autumn, and we were racing headlong into winter. It was late evening, and the jail was quiet because the police were apparently busy with motor-vehicle accidents that resulted from the first snowfall of the winter. From what I heard on the radio, at least two feet of snow had crippled Chicago and Milwaukee.

The book that Pastor Skilton had brought me was getting to look dog-eared and the pages colorful because I had read and marked it so much. Reading for the second or third time, I came across a passage that I had read before, but this time the paragraph had impact.

> By *faith* you became Christ's, and by faith you are to grow up in Him—by giving and taking. You are to *give* all—your heart, your will, your service—give yourself to Him to obey all His requirements; and you must *take* all—Christ, the fullness of all blessing, to abide in your heart, to be your strength, your righteousness, your everlasting helper—to give you power to obey (*Steps to Christ,* p. 70).

This paragraph took my breath away. The feeling was similar to the way I felt standing in the O'Hare Airport, alone and scared because either the detective or I was lost. In absolute desperation I fell to my knees beside the cot and began to sob. I knew what I had to do, and it petrified me. Give it up? Give up my agenda, my plans that I thought were God-inspired for the future? Did I actually have to tell God that I would give up freedom, that I would be willing to go to the pen again if that's what He wanted? Was there someone who needed me there? I'd never been needed in my life, so who could possibly need me now?

And the fight was on! I tried to pray, to say nicely, reverently, that I would be willing . . . but I couldn't. Jacob wrestled with an angel, or was that with God? That's what it felt like. I was fighting for my life, yes, for my life **outside** the prison, not inside! I was struggling to make sense of what felt like absolute senselessness to me. One second I was angry, sweat dripping from me onto the musty blanket on my cot, and the next I was feeling the victim, feeling sorry for myself. Had I ever given up, ever in my life? I usually fought to the bitter end. Surrender? Give up? Be vulnerable? I can't!

But where had my fight-to-the-end attitude gotten me? It had brought me frustration, anguish, anger, sadness, misery. I read the words again: "You are to *give* all—your heart, your will . . ."

Giving up my will was the hard part. I was as strong-willed as they come. I didn't want anyone else, not even God, to determine my future! But I had to admit that I had already messed up my life when I was in control. I hadn't done a very good job of orchestrating my life so far; perhaps letting God take charge would be a good idea.

After a long struggle, I was able to pray: "God, I give up! I give up my desire, my need to be free. I give up my reasoning, because obviously, God, it's not Yours. I give up my hopes, my dreams, and my plans for the future. If You really want me to go up north to the pen for another ten years, for however long, it's OK. I'll do what You want me to do. I'll go where You want me to go. Maybe someone like Ellis needs to hear from someone like me, and maybe to someone like him is where I'll be sent. So I'll go, if You say so. I'm done with the fighting. You're in charge. You're the Boss. I surrender! Amen."

Totally drained, I climbed onto the cot and fell asleep. It was the most peaceful sleep I had in three months. I felt like a baby in the tender, yet powerful arms of its daddy now, because Dad was in charge. He would care for me in the way that He knew was best, and I would let Him. He was in charge again, just as He had been in Nashville and the Adventist services I wanted to attend; as He had been when the guards did not shoot me down for foolishly walking across the compound unescorted; as He had been about the movie on Sabbath; as He had been about keeping me strong after I refused to eat unclean meat—maybe just as He'd always been.

The next morning I was awakened for breakfast at the usual hour. The guard who brought the breakfast said, "Rockey, I'll be bringing your own clothes in a little while, and you can go to the showers if you want to, because you have a court appointment this morning. They'll come for you about 8:45, so you'll need to be ready."

For a second or two I was in shock, and then I said, "Yes, Sir, I would like a shower if I could, and I can assure you that I'll be ready on time. As soon as you bring the clothes, I'll be ready for my shower."

My heart raced as I gulped my breakfast ravenously. I'd probably need to have that food for strength, because only God knew what the day would bring. Strength for another prison? Please God, but . . .

At 8:45 sharp my cell door opened, and I was escorted down several long halls and taken to another locked room where several other prisoners were waiting. I was the only one dressed in street clothes rather than the dungaree shirt and pants I wore in the cell, and I felt a bit conspicuous. "You'll wait here until someone calls your name, and then you'll appear before the judge," I was told. Every twenty minutes or so, a guard would come to the room, unlock the door, and call for one of the prisoners. I sat there praying, mostly for courage.

It was nearly 10:30 by the time the guard called my name. I noticed that the other prisoners were wearing handcuffs when they were called, but I walked out of that room and into the courtroom without those steel bands around my wrists. I was grateful, not because they were so humiliating, but because each time I had to wear them, I would get a terrible headache; that day of all days, I wanted to have a clear, pain-free mind.

The judge sat at an elevated bench made of some type of highly polished dark wood. He looked straight at me and spoke my name. "Yes, Sir," I responded. I stood there at attention with my hands folded behind my back as if I were standing in front of a military tribunal or invisibly handcuffed. For the next few minutes, he reviewed the charges before me and asked a few questions about my Tennessee experiences. I was careful to not tell the gruesome story. Beside him was another file folder that he picked up, and then he kindly ordered me to go and sit at the bench to his right. As I walked toward the bench to sit, I noticed that there was an audience in the courtroom. I wondered if my mother or any of my family was there, but instead I saw my pastor. He sat in the front row and looked straight at me. I wasn't sure why he was there; I didn't see a family member, but I was thrilled to see him. Beside him sat his wife Hazel, a demure little woman with a sweet smile. I nodded and cautiously smiled at her and she responded likewise. I took a deep breath, enjoying the feeling that somebody cared enough to be there for me.

Beside Mrs. Damazo sat a young woman in a burgundy suit. I glanced at her quickly and then took a second look. Who was this? She seemed to be with the Damazos, but she couldn't be their daughter. The pastor had said that he had two daughters still in grade school. She looked at me and smiled, and I returned her smile. I felt drawn to her, felt her acceptance right away. I heard my name being called by the judge and heard the words "approach the bench."

"I have reviewed your case, young man, and it appears that you have made a remarkable change in your life," he said. "Do you have someone here in Milwaukee who can watch over you, be a guide for you?"

"Yes, Sir. I have family and a very wonderful pastor. He is here in the courtroom today for me," I answered.

"Well, then, I've decided to put you on three year's probation. During that time you will have to report to both the Federal Parole Board and the Parole for the State of Wisconsin. These men will explain to you the conditions of your parole. Their names and their office addresses and phone numbers are on this paper you'll need to take with you. I hope, young man, that your change will be a permanent one. Good luck. Case dismissed," he concluded as he banged his gavel on the bench.

I wasn't sure what to do then. I looked to the guard for direction, I suppose with a questioning expression. "You're free to go!" he said.

The court had also been adjourned, so I turned toward the audience and noticed that the pastor and his wife and friend had stood. The pastor put out his arms to me and welcomed me with a hug. Right away, he introduced me to his wife, Hazel. We shook hands and she said that she was so pleased to meet me. Then the pastor introduced me to the young woman beside Hazel. "This is our good friend Nancy," he said. "She has come for a few days to visit us, so we brought her with us this morning. She put her hand out to shake mine, and I responded. As our hands clasped, our eyes met, and my heart leaped. She was blushing, and probably I was too.

"Do you have things that you need to get at the jail, Ron?" the pastor asked.

"Yes, Sir, I do. Just my Bible and *Steps to Christ*. I certainly don't want to leave them behind," I answered.

We found our way back down a set of stairs to the jail. The pastor and I left Mrs. Damazo and Nancy in the lobby and went to the locked jail door. We rang the bell several times before it was answered. The guard looked at us strangely.

"Sir, I've come to get my things from my cell," I said.

"You can't come in here. You've been released!" he said.

It took some convincing to get the guard to let me back to my cell to recover my Bible. The pastor and I went into my old cell and then walked out together for the last time.

"Ron, isn't this funny?" the pastor chuckled when we were outside the locked jail. "Here you've been waiting to get out for so long, and now that you're finally out, they won't even let you in to get your belongings!" It felt so exhilarating to laugh together as we headed toward Hazel and Nancy and toward freedom—at last.

CHAPTER 14

Milwaukee Country Courthouse was located downtown, not far from the icy waters of Lake Michigan. It was almost noontime as we made our way to the Damazo's car. Even though the sun was nearly as high as it would get that day, the temperature was considerably below freezing, and a crisp wind blew off the lake. I was wearing the light-weight suit that had been given to me by the state of Tennessee, but, cold as I was, I didn't care or complain. Finally, I was going to my family, and I had a new friendship to cultivate with the young woman who sat with Hazel in the back seat of the car.

As soon as we got in the vehicle, the pastor turned to me. "Ronnie, this day's for you. Where would you like to go, and what would you like to do?" he inquired. It took only an instant to answer.

"Pastor, I would like to see the church—if it's not too far out of the way, that is," I answered. "I'd like to go inside to see what it's like." The day's events were so wonderful that I felt compelled to go directly to God's house and thank Him.

"That's exactly where we'll go then. It's not far from here at all, right near the lake." The church was the former mansion of A. O. Smith, the great Milwaukee inventor, Pastor Damazo informed me. "It's a beautiful building, and the sanctuary, which is upstairs, is built over what used to be the swimming pool. We have a great church family here, Ronnie, and you'll fit right in," he said. "You'll see."

We went into a huge brick mansion in what I remembered as the affluent side of town. The pastor carefully pointed out details to me, such as the hand-tooled leather wallpaper in the foyer. The pastor led us up a magnificent divided staircase to the sanctuary. The four of us stood in the doorway at the rear, and I just stared for a minute or two. "Mind if I go in for a couple of minutes alone, Pastor?" I asked.

In the quietness of what seemed like the most beautiful place I'd ever seen, I stepped into a pew and fell to my knees. Finally, I was free, and I had to thank my Lord. Finally, I was at home, the dwelling place of my Father.

I was grateful when the pastor asked if I'd like to have some lunch. "We can go to the school and meet our girls for lunch. The school serves wonderful hot vegetarian lunches, and the staff always cooks extra," the pastor said. It didn't matter to me where we went to eat lunch. Anything would be better than what I had eaten for the past few years! I was eager to chat with Nancy, but the pastor kept asking questions about my plans for the future, and in just a few moments we were at the school.

After lunch and a brief tour of the school, I was asked again where I would like to go next. It seemed only right that I should go to see my mother, who hadn't been able to attend the court session because she was working. I gave directions to the pastor, who knew exactly where the Marshall Field's store was where my mother worked. Then I immediately turned around so that I could chat with Nancy, who was in the back seat of the car. I inquired about where she lived and how she knew the Damazos. She told me that she had known them since she was four years old, when he was the pastor at her home church in Connecticut. Her family and the pastor's family had been friends ever since.

Nancy explained that she was a part-time student studying for her bachelor's degree in nursing at a university four hours' drive from Milwaukee. She was also working full time as a campus nurse and was engaged to a young man who was a graduate student at the same university. She and her fiancé were having some relationship difficulties, and she chose to drive the distance to Milwaukee to get some advice from her family friends.

Engaged! What a letdown. I had hoped that I would have a chance with this girl. There was something special about her, and I was intrigued with the fact that she was already a nurse. I felt her compassion, the attitude that I had always assumed a nurse would have, and, besides that, she had beautiful legs! I knew how to appreciate lovely legs, since I had danced professionally. To be honest, in the courtroom it was her legs that I noticed first. She wore a very classy burgundy suit and black high-heeled shoes and carried gloves and a purse. She impressed me as a mature, well-put-together young woman, and I was already setting my sights in her direction.

We talked a bit about her plans for the future, and she asked about mine. I told her that I had felt called to the ministry since becoming a Christian, and that as soon as I was able to, I intended to go to school to prepare myself academically to be a pastor. She told me some about the university she was attending and that in addition to the university, there was a seminary to train pastors.

"Well then, I'll have to get some information about it, I guess, because that's where I'll have to go as soon as possible," I said.

"I'll be happy to get you a school bulletin," she offered. "I can send it to the pastor, and he can give it to you when you see each other in church."

"That's wonderful. Thank you!" I exclaimed.

We pulled up into the huge parking lot of Marshall Field's, and all four of us got out of the car into the windy cold and just about ran into the store. We took the escalator to the second floor, where the bakery was located. At the bakery counter I asked to see Renata Rockey for just a moment and identified myself as her son Ron. While we waited, I pointed out to Nancy the bakery items that I was sure Mother had made, the same ones that I recognized from my childhood years at home. I was drooling; actually, I guess we all were. Nancy bought a few items for the Damazos and one of my favorite pecan sticky buns for me. I thought to myself, "Yup, you were right, Kiddo. She's the one for me!"

Finally Mother came out in her white, flour-covered baker's uniform, complete with hat. She seemed very pleased to see me and gave me a hug for the first time in years. I wondered whether the hug was to impress the pastor. I introduced her to the Damazos and to Nancy. Because Mother could spare only a few minutes from her baking, we chatted briefly. She told me that I could go to Phyllis's house and that she'd be home at four o'clock. As we started back to the escalator, I turned back to Mother and whispered, "See that girl, Ma? I'm going to marry her!" Ma just stared.

Back in the car we chatted more about Nancy's family and about Phyllis, the sister to whose house we were driving. In seemingly no time the pastor pulled in front of Phyllis and Johnny's house. "Well, Son, this is where we part for now," the pastor said. "But here is my card with my phone number. I want you to call me tomorrow, and we'll make plans to get together. Tomorrow night the church is going Ingathering. I doubt that you know what that means, but I'll explain it all to you tomorrow. We will meet at the church at five o'clock for a soup supper, and then we'll go out caroling after that. You make sure to call me tomorrow morning. Now you enjoy your family this evening. We'll wait here to make sure someone is home." The pastor spit out the words so fast, that I hardly had time to say goodbye to Hazel and Nancy.

"See you tomorrow evening, Nancy!" I called out over my shoulder as I ran toward the door of my sister's home. My stomach did a big flip as I rang the bell. I knew the house, but did I know the people in it? Would they want me? Would I be welcomed as a family member?

The door swung open, and Phyllis, holding a baby boy in her arms, was standing there. "Butch!" she hollered. "Come in, come in. It's so good to see you!" I waved goodbye to the people in the car waiting at the curb, and they drove away. There goes the woman of my dreams, I thought. My future is in that car.

Phyllis hadn't changed much since the last time I had seen her except that there was a baby boy now to add to the three girls she and Johnny already had. She told me that Johnny was still working for Miller's Brewery, and Mother was still living in that upstairs bedroom. "We got a bed ready for you for just in case they let you out," she said. "Now sit and tell me about this morning, about what's been happening to you. You seem different."

Phyllis ironed as we talked. She kept trying to give me something to eat, but I wasn't hungry. Even though I was conversing with Phyl, my heart and part of my head were following a certain green Chrysler.

The next morning I slept until ten o'clock, and it felt so good not to be wakened by clanging bars or screaming guards. As soon as I woke up, I went downstairs, and Phyl poured me some orange juice. "How many eggs do you want?" During home leaves from the navy, I had been used to eating a dozen, scrambled.

"Two would be great, Phyl, but I can fix them," I said. Phyl was shocked and quickly reminded me of the old days when a dozen was about right. I had changed, and I had made up my mind to change even more. While Phyllis fixed the eggs, I called the pastor. We made arrangements for him to pick me up later in the day for whatever it was that the church folk were going to do that evening.

At the church tables set up in the fellowship hall for our soup supper, I looked around but did not see Nancy. Hazel asked if she could help; she said I looked puzzled. I told her that I hadn't seen Nancy there and asked where she was. "Oh, she's gone back to the university. She left this morning, Ronnie." My heart sank. I really hadn't come out that night to eat soup and do whatever it was that the folks were going to do. I had come to be with Nancy.

Two weeks later at church, Pastor Damazo handed me a large manila envelope addressed to me at his address. "I believe this is the university catalogue Nancy promised to send," he said. I thanked him and went off by myself to open the envelope, hoping that there might be a note from her. I was pleased that she had written a brief note saying that this was the material she had promised me, that she had been pleased to meet me, and that she would keep me in her prayers as I prepared to come to the university.

A couple more weeks passed, and I was lonely. I had noticed another young woman in the church and decided to get acquainted with her. We had several dates and I was enjoying the opportunity to visit with a female and to feel human again. But I couldn't put aside my thoughts of Nancy and my dream that one day she would be my wife.

Christmas came and went, and so did the New Year's holiday. It was the last Sabbath of January, and already I was involved helping out at the church. On this particular day, I was greeting folks at the door and giving out the church bulletin. The heavy oak door opened, and I was shocked to see Nancy walk into the lobby. "Nancy! How good to see you! What are you doing here?" I asked.

"I came to visit the pastor and his wife," she replied.

"Yes, but **why** did you come?" I persisted.

"I guess you knew that I was engaged. Well, the engagement is broken, and I've just come to get away for a few days," she answered sheepishly.

"It is? Oh, it is? I'm sorry. Can we sit together in church?" I jumped right in.

We sat together through the first study service and then for the worship hour. She sang that day just before the pastor's sermon, and I thought that I'd never heard anything so beautiful. I was truly smitten, and I knew it. "Thank You, thank You," I said over and over during the prayer time and in between. Now I'll have a chance to keep my prediction made to Mother. "Please, God. Please let her be mine," I prayed.

When the service was over, we went down the staircase to the foyer, where we stood talking to people we both knew. Nancy happened to turn her head in the direction of the divided staircase where the pastor and his wife stood greeting the members as they came down to the foyer. Suddenly she grabbed my arm and pointed toward the pastor. "There's my father!" she exclaimed as she hurried in that direction. I followed her, as surprised and confused as she was. Her parents lived in Connecticut. What was her father doing in Milwaukee? Of course Nancy hugged her dad, and then, stepping back from him, she asked, "Dad, what are you doing here?"

"Well, Poode," he said, "I came to console you, but it doesn't look like you need much consolation. Who's he?" he asked as he looked upward at me.

"Oh, Dad, I'm fine. And this is Ron Rockey. He's such a nice young man. He just came out of prison, and I met him here in Milwaukee a few months ago." I shook hands with her father, and I wondered if this would be the abrupt end to my dream.

I was later invited to the Damazos' house for an evening worship and ice cream to follow. We sang hymns standing around their piano, with Nancy's dad at the keyboard. Boy, could he play! I was mesmerized. As soon as the worship ended, Nancy's father asked if he could use the phone to call his wife in Connecticut. He wanted her to know that he had arrived safely in Milwaukee and that he had found Nancy. He talked for a few moments and then called Nancy to the phone. I followed her and stood nearby as she chatted with her mother. "Oh, I am really OK, Mom. I've just met the most wonderful young man. He just came out of prison, and we've been having a great evening here at the Damazos!"

I knew she had said too much. In seconds she handed the phone back to her father. We stood nearby as he listened to his wife. Finally, I heard him say, "That's enough, Ena. When a man is born in Christ, he is a new creature. Old things are passed away, and all has become new. I will not listen to another word. Do you understand me?"

The conversation ended in another minute, and not another word was spoken about it. But Nancy's dad looked knowingly at me as he hung up the phone. And from his look, I received a very powerful message.

As I went home that night, I thought to myself, I've left Nashville and Leonard, the only man I've ever recognized as a father. But tonight I have found a real father. Not only has the door to a relationship with Nancy been opened, but I also have found one who has accepted me with no strings attached. He will be what I need to encourage me to pursue my goals. And one day, maybe when he's really my father, he'll say the words I heard tonight in his silent glance of love.

EPILOGUE

Nancy and I have been married for thirty-six years. These have been years of training, years of refining, and years of preparation for the work that God had planned all along that we would do for Him. Not all of these years were pleasant; we both experienced much pain and suffering during the early years of our marriage, and all too much of it was dumped upon the two beautiful miracle daughters we were blessed with.

I look back today to my beginnings, some of which I do not remember in detail. Other family members have filled in some of the blanks of early childhood; they have reported the facts as they saw them, and that has helped me to confirm the feelings of rejection I have felt all of my life. I think back to becoming a husband, and I realize that I was ill-prepared for what was to come: parenting, pastoring, and enduring added pain. I could do only what I had seen done; I could love only out of my emptiness.

Yet, this one thing I do know. All along the way, from the moment that I was conceived to this very hour, God has never once removed His love and His calling on my life. Even in the depths of "the hole," even in the quagmire of my sinful ways, my rebellion, my anger, my need to be in control of my life and everyone else's, God has never turned His back, but has steadfastly walked with me through the muck—and perhaps at times even carried me on His shoulders. From my very beginnings, He has longed to be the Father mine couldn't be, the one I needed so much that I was willing to sacrifice eternity, to guarantee eternity for him.

In the midst of my rebellion, I could not see that His hand was upon me, and that He sent surrogate fathers to be to me just what I needed at the time. Hindsight is always 20/20 I'm told, and hindsight reveals all the men, all the proxy fathers who have walked alongside, supporting me, loving and encouraging me, until I could catch a glimpse of the Father who has never left me. To Him, my true Father, and to all the "fathers" along the way, I am abundantly grateful!

Ron's birth father, Stanley C. Rockey.

Leonard C. Haswell, God's instrument to bring more than 500 men to Christ. Notice the similarity of his appearance to Ron's father, Stanley Rockey.

Ron's "real" father, his father-in-law, James Hallas.

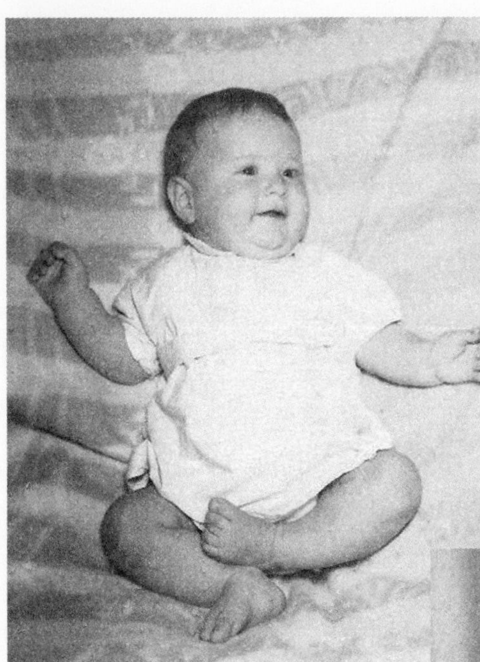

Ron at about 3 months of age.

Ron had long curly hair and wore dresses until he was about 3 1/2.

Ron at age 8. This photo was taken after the move to Wakasha Road.

Ron at age 13 showing visible anger. Rebellion is firmly in place at this point.

Ron at about age 16 with Johnny, Phyllis's husband.

Ron, the tough young sailor, in Spain.

The USS Fremont.

The gate through which Ron walked
when he escaped from Shelby County Correctional Facility.

Ron in a classroom of the Federal Penitentiary in El Reno, Oklahoma.

Ron giving a speech at a Toastmaster's ceremony in the Federal Penitentiary at El Reno, Oklahoma.

The castle-like front entrance to the "big house."

Nashville State Penitentiary housed 5000 prisoners, a self-contained town. The enormous facility was condemned while Ron was still incarcerated there, but it functioned as the state prison for an additional 25 years. The facility no longer houses prisoners but remains standing and is occasionally used as the site of movie shoots.

Ron was housed for several months in Nashville State Penitentiary's tri-level cell-block.

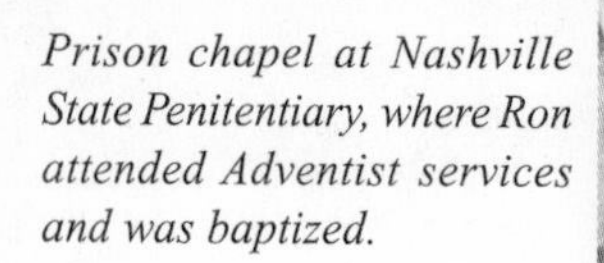

Prison chapel at Nashville State Penitentiary, where Ron attended Adventist services and was baptized.

Classification center where all prisoners entering the Nashville State Penitentiary were housed for thirty days. During that time the men were fingerprinted and photographed, their backgrounds were checked, files were created, and the men were classified as to their risk potential. Ron worked here and was housed in a privileged area with Reuben because of their good prison records.

Ron took and developed this self-portrait while in federal prison.

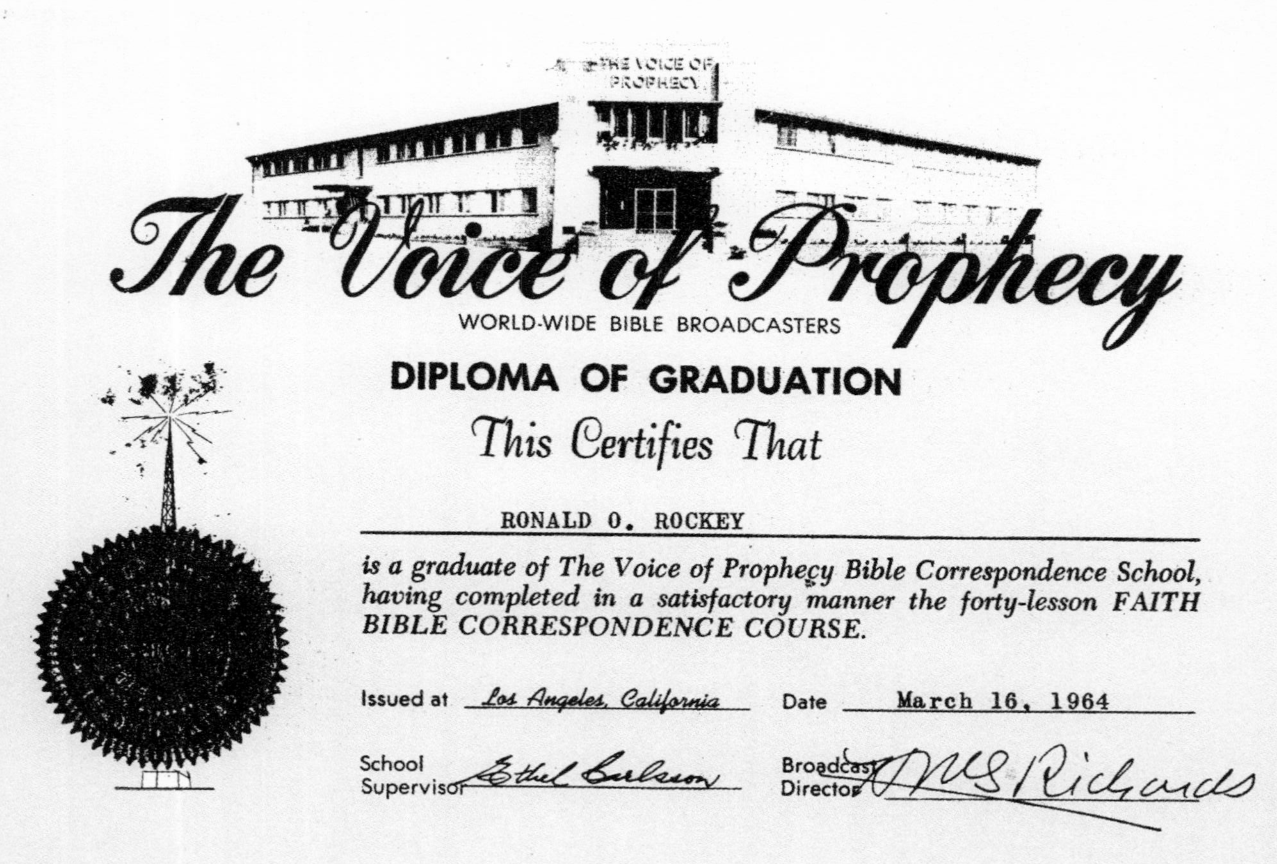
The Voice of Prophecy

WORLD-WIDE BIBLE BROADCASTERS

DIPLOMA OF GRADUATION

This Certifies That

RONALD O. ROCKEY

is a graduate of The Voice of Prophecy Bible Correspondence School, having completed in a satisfactory manner the forty-lesson FAITH BIBLE CORRESPONDENCE COURSE.

Issued at Los Angeles, California Date March 16, 1964

School Supervisor Broadcast Director

Bible course certificate from The Voice of Prophecy earned while Ron was incarcerated in Nashville State Penitentiary.

Diploma of Bible Study

This certifies that RONALD O. ROCKEY

has completed in a satisfactory manner the

series of lessons as outlined in the

Faith for Today Bible Course

In witness whereof we have hereunto affixed our signatures

Issued at New York, N. Y. on this 4TH day of SEPTEMBER 19 64

Bible School Pastor

Director

Bible course certificate from Faith For Today earned while Ron was incarcerated in Nashville State Penitentiary.

Pastor Joseph S. Damazo,
Ron's friend and mentor after he was released to Milwaukee
from Nashville State Penitentiary.

Leonard C. Haswell congratulating "his boy" at Ron's ordination.

Ron and Leonard Haswell in June 1977, during the weekend of Ron's ordination.

Physical and psychological well-being begin at conception. Modern medical science is discovering the importance of the atmosphere surrounding the child in the womb. These are some recent discoveries:

1. Scientists suspect that an embryo as young as forty-eight hours following conception can sense rejection and has sufficient intelligence to act on it.

2. It has been determined that the circumstance with the most profound effect on the child in the womb is the relationship between the pregnant mother and the man who impregnated her.

3. Beginning at the fourth month of pregnancy, the feelings and emotions of the mother are directly transferred to the child in the womb, and the child records them as his/her own (Thomas Verney, M.D., *The Secret Life of the Unborn Child*).

For the first year or so of life, children do not use spoken language. However, they interpret voice inflections, tone and pitch, facial expressions, and body language, and are very sensitive to emotional upsets. During this time, the brain's neurons are forming pathways that inevitably become habits or modes of thinking, and the mind is at its most vulnerable, absorbing information through all senses and through emotions.

During the first year of life, babies learn 50 percent of everything they will ever learn, and in the second year, they learn an additional 25 percent. These early lessons are the foundation, the framework for the formation of the thoughts and feelings of the future adult. What infants learn from their parents, their primary caregivers, becomes the value system upon which future decisions are made.

When a baby is ignored or feels unwanted, it is programmed to experience emotional poverty. "The disease of emotional poverty creates its own appetite for powerful sensation. The deadness within becomes the source of an intolerable tension, quite simply . . . the ultimate terror of non-being, the dissolution of self. The deadness within demands at times powerful psychic jolts in order to affirm existence" (Selma Fraiberg, *Every Child's Birthright: In Defense of Mothering,* Basic Books). Is it any wonder that we are inundated with news reports of road rage, violent murders, and rapes?

How blessed we are that we have a surrogate Parent, One who can provide for us far beyond what we would ever dream or desire. It we allow it, He can and will become the Acceptance, the Comfort, and the Stability of our present experience. The first step in allowing Him to provide for us is to acknowledge the pain that we have endured; we must name the pain. Then, using biblical tools for healing wounded hearts and relationships, the old pain can be expelled, and we can allow ourselves to be filled with Christ's presence.

If you didn't have a whole and healthy home in childhood, take this one lesson for today and always: Home is the presence of the Father.

You can be at home—a better home than you ever dreamed possible—if you simply are willing to be emptied of painful emotions and make room for your heavenly Father to dwell within you.

From birth I was cast upon you;
from my mother's womb you have been my God
(Psalm 22:10).

PSALM 27:10

LESSON 2

For every effect there is a cause. Scripture tells us that we are to train up a child in the way he should go (the cause) and when he is old, he will not depart from it (the effect) (see Proverbs 22:6). When children receive all of the emotional nutrients they require to be emotionally and physically healthy, they will be healthy. But if they lack necessary emotional nutrients, the deficiency will be demonstrated by psychological or physical symptoms throughout life—during infancy, childhood, and adult years.

Current studies indicate the strong influence of the right brain in a child from birth to age three. The right brain is commonly known to be the sensitive, visionary, creative side of the brain.

A growing body of studies shows that the infant's early maturing (Geschwin and Galaburda, 1987) right hemisphere is specifically impacted by early social experiences. (Schore, 1994, 1998b).

This developmental principle is now supported in a recent single photon emission computed tomographic (SPECT) study by Chiron et al. (1997), which demonstrates that the right brain hemisphere is dominant in preverbal human infants and for the first three years of life. This ontogenetic (developmental) shift of dominance from the right to left hemisphere at this time may explicate Bowlby's description of a diminution (progressive decrease) of the attachment system at the end of the third year that is due to an "abrupt" passage of a "maturational threshold." (From "Studies on the Neurobiology of Attachment" in the book *Attachment* by John Bowlby. Basic Books, 1969, 1982.)

Every child's primary need is for a mother and father to be present both physically and emotionally. We know that empathy (understanding, sympathy, compassion) is developed by the end of a child's third year of life, and it is developed by the modeling of mother and father's empathy demonstrated toward each other and toward the child. This would assist the child, if positively developed, to be other-centered rather than self-centered (narcissistic).

In Bowlby's second volume (1973), he refines the set-goal of the attachment system as "not just proximity but access to an attachment figure who is emotionally available and responsive" (Forward to *Attachment* by John Bowlby, written by Allan N. Schole).

This need for a father and mother is so basic that a child deprived will suffer instability for a lifetime and will usually seek for someone, usually a marital partner, who will fill for him or her the emptiness left by the physically or emotionally absent parent(s).

The divinely appointed father's role is to be provider and protector, and when the father takes this role seriously, the child feels safe, stable, secure, and loved. A child needs an emotional bond with the father, needs to have verbal and physical assurance of acceptance and love, constancy, and words of affirmation. Actually, the parents stand in the place of God to a young child (see Ellen G. White, *Signs of the Times,* May 14, 1894).

If mother and father are unable or unwilling to provide the emotional security and the acceptance on which children build their concept of self, children will develop a negative, deficient sense of self. They will see their personal worth and value as inferior, will have little interest in developing or recognizing abilities, will see life as not worth living, and may fail to thrive, a condition in which children become emaciated and despondent and die. All too often, if such children physically survive childhood, they will become emotionally dwarfed underachievers. Other children respond with the opposite extreme. They can be so driven to prove their value and worth that they focus entirely on the pursuit of work and success.

Children who are blessed with a physically and emotionally present set of parents who adore each other, are excited about their children's births, and welcome their presence are given a great initiation to life. Time, attention to emotional and physical needs, and affectionate touch all combine to give an infant the greatest possible jump-start to a happy and successful life.

The great news is that even if you lacked a sound beginning, during your adult life you can learn to be happy and productive and to benefit yourself and bless others. Regardless of the father in your family of origin, your heavenly Father longs to make Himself known to you. As you will or have discovered in Ron's story, He will do whatever is necessary to convey His love and concern to you. He will bring into your life people who will temporarily fill the vacancies in your heart with the kind of love and direction that you need. He will watch brokenheartedly as you choose paths that are destructive; and all the while He will be calling you to Himself, knowing full well that sometimes the pain screams so loudly within you that you cannot hear His voice.

And when you finally turn to Him because there is no one else who can help, the best Father there is can so transform your present experiences that the pain is removed from your memories of the past; and they then become the steppingstones to a brighter tomorrow.

Though my father and mother forsake me,
the Lord will receive me
(Psalm 27:10).

ISAIAH 43:1

LESSON 3

We know that rejected kids are the ones most vulnerable to further abuse. They so long to connect with another person that they are unconscious of the seductive behaviors of perpetrators. It's a set-up, part of Satan's agenda to see that children are damaged, so that they'll grow up to be damaged adults and then pass on the pain to their children and grandchildren and anyone else around them. Human beings were designed to connect with others and especially with their Creator, and we long to do so. Unfortunately for many, the connection that takes place is not nurturing and constructive, but hurtful and destructive.

Children's basic emotional task is to develop trust. According to the psychologist Eric Erickson, trust is developed during the first eighteen months of life. It is based on the trust relationship children have with their primary caregivers, the parents. The second emotional task is to develop autonomy—the ability to govern oneself or to make decisions. In order to be able to develop step two adequately, trust must first have been established.

Ron developed neither adequately. As a result, he developed a certain amount of self-trust, but a conflicting message sabotaged the self-trust he had. He knew that he had to trust himself because there was no one else to count on. The derogatory words he had heard from his father conflicted with his self-trust. While his mind told him that he was the only one he could trust, the emotional memories formed by hearing criticism from authority figures (parents) told him that he was inadequate and a failure.

When significant losses take place in the character-forming years (conception through the seventh year of life), the tendency is to predict and prepare for losses throughout the remainder of life. If the individual later develops fulfilling and intimate relationships, they would contradict the foundational experiences. This contradiction creates the need to sabotage the relationships in order to feel comfortable or "normal."

Sometimes our beginnings, difficult and painful though they are, can be used by God to comfort or help heal others with painful pasts. The pain was not in God's plan, but the empathy or wisdom that grew out of the painful experiences can be used in God's service. Because we cannot foretell the future, we cannot imagine how God can bring any good out of these experiences. But eventually we will be able to look back and see how God was able to make something useful from our experiences.

Ron's lonely childhood and rejection by his father would give him resources that would help prepare him for solitary years to come—years when death seemed a better option than life, when friends proved unfaithful, when imprisonment brought isolation, and when vocation would place him in a lonely pulpit.

Perhaps you feel isolated, that you belong to no one. Isaiah 43:1 is a text of consolation and comfort. Here God tells you that He has called you by name, a pet name at that, and that you are His. To know that you belong to a nurturing, compassionate, understanding Father is for many the greatest comfort possible. It remains Ron's greatest comfort and joy!

This is what the Lord says—
he who created you, . . .
he who formed you, . . .
"Fear not, for I have redeemed you;
I have summoned you by name; you are mine"
(Isaiah 43:1).

ISAIAH 49:15, 16

LESSON 4

Have you ever felt that you were an unwelcome guest in a place where you were visiting? Pretty uncomfortable, isn't it? Imagine feeling that way every day of your life in the place that houses your bed, your clothes, and your family. What must it feel like to be constantly wishing that you were somewhere else with someone who showed you some attention or consideration? Can you recall a time in your life when you overheard others talking against you and wishing that you were not a part of their experience? That awful realization that you are not wanted, not accepted, and not approved of was how Ron felt every day of his childhood.

Rejection causes the severest emotional damage of all. It is what Satan feels because he is rejected. Of course the Bible tells us that Satan's rejection is the inevitable result of his own choice to reject God's authority. It's been the name of his game ever since the creation of humankind. The Bible also tells us that Jesus Christ "was despised and rejected by men, a man of sorrows, and familiar with suffering. Like one from whom men hide their faces he was despised, and we esteemed him not" (Isaiah 53:3).

Rejection creates within its victims a false self-image. They reason, "I must be garbage, worthless, if those who created me don't love me." Rejected individuals find themselves to be incapable of establishing or maintaining intimacy in a friendship or in marriage. For them, everyone is suspect; everyone has the potential to abandon, to ignore, to expect performance in exchange for acceptance, or to cause further pain by ultimately rejecting them. This desperation creates a sense of loneliness that feels to its victim like they are stuck deep inside a well out in the middle of nowhere with no one to rescue them.

> Loneliness is like the Grand Canyon. It engulfs a person and makes him or her feel totally insignificant. It seems to wrap around a person because of its enormity and makes a person feel totally insignificant. Loneliness only recedes when we finally find someone in these deep crevices to connect with and talk to (author unknown).

Repeated experiences of early rejection, such as a mother who might be physically present but emotionally absent from her child, strip the child of the experience of being a part of or significant in another's life. In adulthood, such people may be friendly, attentive, or enjoyable to be around, but they usually lack the ability to share their inner personhood. While the need to connect emotionally is great for such individuals, in intimate relationships they feel awkward, even abused, and often push their partner away.

Ron's experience of rejection began while he was still in the womb, taking in his mother's fears and denial of his existence until the end of her pregnancy, and this rejection continued throughout infancy and childhood. Later in life, its influence led him into a life of rebellion to all authority, resulting in his incarceration.

Studies Regarding Prenatal Influence

Numerous studies have shown the effect on the fetus by negative events (both physical and emotional) in the mother's life. Studies also reveal long-term effects of maternal rejection of the fetus.

- The fetus has been found to be sensitive to a wide range of maternal emotions, in addition to any drugs or other physical traumas the mother endures.
- When the mother feels anxiety, her increased heartbeat, frightened speech, and alterations in neurotransmitter levels are instantly communicated to the fetus, and her tachycardia (rapid heart rate) is followed within seconds by the fetus's tachycardia. When she feels fear,

within 50 seconds the fetus can be made hypoxic (low on oxygen).

- Alterations in adrenaline, plasma epinephrine, and norepinephrine levels, high levels of hydroxycortico-steriods, hyperventilation, and many other products of maternal anxiety are also known to directly affect the human fetus. Numerous other studies document sensory, hormonal, and biochemical mechanisms by which the fetus is in communication with the mother's feelings and with the outside world.
- Positive maternal emotions have been experimentally shown to increase later growth, alertness, calmness, and intelligence (the fetus even benefits from the mother singing to it in the womb). Prenatal infant stimulation, particularly being bathed in pleasant music, improves fetal development compared to control groups.
- Maternal distress and chemical toxins have been shown to produce low birth weights, increased infant mortality, respiratory infections, asthma, and reduced cognitive development.
- Ultrasound studies record fetal distress clearly, as it thrashes about and kicks in pain during hypoxia and other conditions. One mother whose husband had just threatened her verbally with violence came into the doctor's office with the fetus thrashing and kicking so violently as to be painful to her, with an elevated heart rate that continued for hours.
- The same wild thrashing has been seen in mothers whose spouses have died suddenly. Maternal fright can actually cause the death of the fetus, and death of the husband and other severe emotional distress within the family during the mother's pregnancy has been associated with fetal damage in large samples in several countries.
- Marital discord between spouses has been correlated "with almost 100 per cent certainty . . . with child morbidity in the form of ill-health, neurological dysfunction, developmental lags, and behavior disturbance."
- Margaret Fries has conducted forty-year longitudinal studies predicting emotional patterns that remain quite constant throughout the lives of those studied and correlated them to the mother's attitude toward the fetus during pregnancy.

- Maternal emotional stress, hostility toward the fetus, and fetal distress have also been statistically correlated in various studies with more premature births, lower birth weights, more neonate neurotransmitter imbalances, more clinging-infant patterns, more childhood psychopathology, more physical illness, higher rates of schizophrenia, lower IQ in early childhood, greater school failure, higher delinquency, and greater propensity as an adult to use drugs, commit violent crimes, and commit suicide.
- This increase in social violence due to pre- and perinatal conditions has recently been confirmed by a major Danish study showing that boys of mothers who do not want to have them (25 percent of pregnant mothers admit they do not want their babies) experience birth complications and are four times as likely when they become teenagers to commit violent crimes than control groups.
- Studies also show similar higher violent crime rates correlated with maternal rejection during pregnancy.

(These studies were sited in a speech given by Dr. Lloyd DeMause as the keynote address at the Seventh International Congress of the Association for Pre- and Perinatal Psychology and Health in San Francisco, California, September 29, 1995.)

These and other studies help us to understand some of the correlation between hurting individuals and the prevalence of crime. The studies help to explain why so many who feel rejected, unloved, or forsaken then strike out at others to make them suffer similar pain.

Notice in Ron's story how he was always sent away from the home when anything stressful or emotional was going to take place i.e., his dog being put to sleep, his cat and kittens being drowned, the funeral of his buddy Tommy, and the moving van being loaded with their furniture. Notice also his need later in the story to escape when circumstances closed him in or felt threatening. The great need to be accepted and to be loved was so beautifully filled by the way Nancy's father accepted him, regardless of his being an ex-con recently released from prison.

Regardless of your beginnings, the best Father there is has a message for you:

Can a mother forget the baby at her breast
and have no compassion on
the child she has borne?
Though she may forget,
I will not forget you!
See, I have engraved you on
the palms of my hands
(Isaiah 49:15, 16).

PSALM 147:3

LESSON 5

Rejection is many things. It is a feeling of not belonging. It is an emotional knowledge that one is not loved or wanted by one or both parents. It is a self-defeating feeling of hopelessness that comes from damage that occurred during prenatal and early childhood years. It is a depressing feeling of not belonging that pervades every moment and every association of life.

In Ron's case, rejection began while he was still in the womb, when his mother feared her husband's rage when he discovered that she was pregnant. Renata's response was probably a combination of her temperament and her life experiences. She denied the obvious pregnancy until it terminated with Ron's birth, and then she fell into a psychosis that allowed her to live out of touch with reality.

Since it is true that the thoughts and feelings of the pregnant mother are transferred to the child in the womb, Ron received the message that he didn't exist. After birth, that message was reinforced when he was ignored most of the time.

Remember how it felt in elementary school to raise your hand and to keep it up for a long time, but the teacher called on everyone else? Do you recall how it feels today to go into a department store to make a purchase, but you can't get a salesperson to wait on you because he or she is busy chatting with someone else? It feels a whole lot worse to be a child in a home in which the oldest daughter gets all of the attention, the second daughter gets all the work and hand-me-downs from the eldest, the next son gets regular beatings, and you are ignored as if you weren't there.

To a son, a father is the model of the man he will become. If the father is either physically or emotionally absent, the son lacks the model needed to discover his masculinity, his manhood. A boy without a father lacks one of the strongest forces necessary to discover his own sexual identity. When a father is distant or absent, the son is left with a hole in his emotions where his father should have been, and that hole is filled with resentment, guilt, mourning for unfulfilled dreams about a relationship, and mistrust. The presence of these negative feelings twists or distorts the God-given law written within the mind to honor one's father.

Without a father in his life, a boy lacks a sense of an internal structure. His ideas are often confused, he has trouble setting goals for himself, and he tends to be indecisive about identifying his own needs. If his mother remains as his only model, he runs the risk of remaining a little boy in relation to his powerful mother.

Lack of a father as a role model, either from rejection or absence, has an expensive price tag! Behavior profiles can accurately predict how both children and teenagers/adults will respond throughout life to early and/or continued rejection.

CHILDHOOD BEHAVIORS

- Is not cuddly with parents
- Treats siblings or animals cruelly
- Lacks eye contact with parents
- Is destructive of property
- Experiences developmental lags
- Shows indiscriminate affection with strangers
- Is superficially engaging and charming
- Lacks cause-to-effect thinking
- Is a loner, bully, controller
- Engages in stealing and lying; lacks a healthy conscience
- Asks nonsense questions, chatters incessantly, or isolates
- Uses abnormal speech patterns
- Hoards or gorges on food
- Has poor impulse control

- Is preoccupied with fire, blood, or gore

TEENAGE BEHAVIORS

- Develops an argumentative attitude
- Seeks friends that parents disapprove of
- Uses disrespectful or bad language
- Has facial expressions that constantly reflect anger or avoidance
- Has repeated absences from church or school
- Has lower academic achievement
- Resists discussing or agreeing on almost any subject
- Is cold and unresponsive to parents' touch
- Avoids parents
- Often turns away in parents' presence
- Shows lack of respect for parents' advice
- Is highly critical of parents
- Indulges in sexual behavior, alcohol, or drugs

Referring back to Ron's teen years, it is easy to see that he exhibited the behaviors listed above. All too often, parents, teachers, and others interpret these behaviors as indicators of a "bad kid," but in reality they are demonstrations of a hurting teen.

All is *not* hopeless! Parents who are willing to look at their personal damage, who are willing to acknowledge the hurt they may have caused their child are taking a giant step toward recovering their offspring. As parents choose to recover from the damage they have received, their thoughts and feelings become healthier, and, as a result, their behaviors will also improve, benefiting their children, regardless of the children's age. Even adult children who are miles away from their parents can sense a switch in the attitudes and behaviors of their parents through phone calls and in letters from their parents.

How do we know that the damage can be healed? There are two reasons:

1. God has promised it.

Remember the story of the children of Israel in the land of Egypt? You can find it in Exodus 12:1-13. God promised that if the fathers would believe in the "blood" being sufficient to cover their sins and would place it on the doorposts of their homes, the death angel would pass over their houses, leaving the children of the faithful fathers alive. Remember, Dad didn't have to weed out the children, leaving the rebellious ones outside. His faith covered the children, the good and the not-so-good ones! (See *Selected Messages,* bk. 3, p. 314.) As it was in the days of the children of Israel, so it is today. Your heavenly Father wants you saved, and your children, all of them, with you!

2. We have experienced it with our own children.

As we have chosen the path of recovery, as we have emptied ourselves of the bitterness, anger, and resentments we harbored, God has found room in our hearts for His Spirit to dwell. He has spoken and demonstrated His love for our children through us, and as a result, they have opened themselves to the same indwelling of God in their hearts and lives!

[The Lord] heals the brokenhearted
and binds up their wounds
(Psalm 147:3).

ISAIAH 54:10

LESSON 6

The emotional pain resulting from a single incident, or worse yet, a lifetime of rejection, is very great. Dr. Joseph Evoy is a psychologist who spent thirty-two years studying adults who reported that rejection was their most pressing issue. He found that rejected people are locked in a mind-prison for a lifetime if there is no intervention to help that individual escape from the trap that rejection sets.

Some rejected individuals behave in manners designed to camouflage any evidence of their emotions; others flaunt their emotions in an attempt to force others to relate to them. We do know some consistent characteristics of people who report feelings of rejection stemming from the relationships with parents:

- Have low self-evaluations
- Endeavor to disprove low self-evaluation
- Have a need to hide the true self
- Experience fear in many forms
- Suffer guilt and depression
- Harbor fear and anxiety
- Express or internalize anger, hostility, and aggression

Joseph Evoy observes that, "a significant background consideration that seems pertinent here is that each person's overall parent-child relationship seems to constitute something of a psychological mold that forms a characteristic pattern for relating to other people that persists for the rest of life."

The rejected individual's hunger for love, acceptance, and approval exists side by side with paralyzing anxiety—fear that rejection will re-occur. As a result, there is frequently a need within to test the trustworthiness of others, as if the rejected person repeatedly asks the question: "What will I have to do for this person to reject me too?"

Ron admits that most of the behaviors listed above are very familiar to him, and at one time or another, they were mechanism he used to survive. He became an alcoholic at a very young age, finding liquor readily available at home. The result—numbing the emotional pain of his rejection—was, in his view, well worth the price he paid to obtain the numbing agent.

When Charles Ward succeeded in having Ron released from the brig, Ron was able to put his need for alcohol on hold for a short period of time. Why? Because Charles provided him with desperately needed acceptance that temporarily overshadowed the excessive pain of his past. Short-term though their relationship was, Charles provided the important model that Ron had been deprived of in his character-forming years. To Charles, Ron must have seemed nonteachable, yet the kindness Charles offered and the example he set had a huge impact. Eventually, after suffering the consequences of his choices, Ron was led to follow Charlie's modeling.

"Though the mountains be shaken
and the hills be removed,
yet my unfailing love for you
will not be shaken . . ."
says the Lord, who has compassion on you
(Isaiah 54:10).

PSALM 139:7-9

LESSON 7

When a parent (or other significant authority figure) disappoints a child, is abusive, or is emotionally absent, the child builds up a reservoir of anger that may be expressed overtly or hidden beneath a mask of performance until the child can no longer hold the pain. It is impossible to predict the day or the circumstance that will cause the emotional dam to burst, sending torrents of uncontrollable rage to drench anyone around. Some can hold these pools of resentment for years, and only occasional hairline cracks will appear, oozing sarcasm, hostile humor, or cynicism onto unsuspecting victims.

In Joseph Evoy's book *The Rejected,* he states: "Clinical evidences support the position that negative feelings such as anger frequently go below consciousness and accumulate there." For the rejected, "intense anger also seemed to carry at least the connotation of injustice—the feeling that something unfair had been perpetrated on them."

Stories abound of kids whose dam finally broke, and the rage, hidden for years behind silent and sometimes intellectual walls, finally explodes in a last violent act of murder and/or suicide. One thirteen-year-old boy had stored so much anger that he shot his father in the back of the head, waited for his mother to come home, and shot her with the rest of the bullets in his gun, screaming, "I love you, I love you!"

Again quoting Joseph Evoy: "Anger resulting from perceived person-caused actions or omissions also appeared to carry a strong retaliatory inclination towards *specific* persons."

For Ron, only a small puddle of resentment built up, because he regularly let his anger flow in every imaginable way. Can you imagine being gutsy enough to confront the warden of the prison in which you are incarcerated? Can you imagine walking out the front gate of that prison while waving at the guards, after warning the warden that you were going to do it? It was as if he was paying back his father for the years of being ignored, being put down, and feeling unloved. Ron's actions were saying, "This time, I'll walk away from you, from the inhuman treatment, from the punishment; I'll reject you, and you can just see how it feels!" These must have been his unconscious motivations.

All the while Ron was pumped up on the adrenaline that anger produces. He was living life on the edge, scared of nothing, conjuring up grandiose plans and attempting to carry them out. He was walking on the edge of life, because life held no meaning. Death would have been a welcome escape from the repeated rejections of his life.

What Ron did not understand, what he was unaware of, was that all along he was being carefully watched by a Father who was saddened by his rage and hopeful for his future. What Ron did not know and certainly couldn't conceive of was that there was a Dad who saw that Ron's negative experiences could uniquely equip him for a ministry, for a life he could not have dreamed possible. Ron might have been able to escape from the stone-and-barbed-wire confinement of a prison; he might have been able to turn his back on those who had turned their backs on him during the early years of his life—but he could not run or hide from the destiny that his Father had planned.

Our heavenly Father follows His children everywhere, offering guidance out of any hiding place. The psalmist expressed confidence in God's persistent presence in Psalm 139.

Where can I go from your Spirit?
Where can I flee from your presence?
If I go up to the heavens, you are there;
if I make my bed in the depths, you are there.
If I rise on the wings of the dawn,
if I settle on the far side of the sea,
even there your hand will guide me,
your right hand will hold me fast
(Psalm 139:7-10).

PSALM 139:1-6

LESSON 8

Dr. Joseph Evoy uses the subject of his many years of research as the title for one of his books—*The Rejected.* In it he made this statement about the long-term consequences of early rejection: "In the rejected, where this ingredient of authentic parental love was withheld, their hunger for it continued unabated through life. Indeed, the rejected had an abiding experience of emptiness which never ceased crying out to be filled."

When we place the characteristic behaviors and experiences of the rejected in perspective against a meaningful background of what their experiences should have been, we have a better understanding of their angst. All children are entitled to life's necessities: food, shelter, protection, and nourishing love. Indeed, warm and personal love from parents is essential to children's physical, emotional, and spiritual well-being. It's from this love that they come to understand the love of a heavenly Father whom they cannot see. More important, what children see and experience from earthly parents, especially the father, is the model for what they will expect from God.

Parental rejection also becomes the blueprint from which each succeeding relationship in life will be patterned. In other words, the rejected expect rejection from others, and they usually get what they anticipate. Moreover, if they do not sense rejection, they will search until they find it, a bit like a dog that searches for a bone it has buried and will not stop until it finds and digs up the bone. Once the expected rejection is found, the rejected "settles in" as a dog will take his "treasure" to his favorite hideout and will contentedly settle in to enjoying it.

The rejected will take the rejection they find into their special hiding place, even if that place is only a mental hiding place, and there will feel the comfort from finally receiving what they thought they deserved and had come to expect. To be sure, the contentment is not from enjoying the rejection, but from experiencing again what has become familiar, even secure.

The constant longing to fill a gnawing emptiness eventually leads the rejected to the sad state of hopelessness. The rejected respond to their despair with behaviors designed to prove that they are worthy of love and have intrinsic worth and value. Teenage boys seek recognition from peers through these behaviors:

- Athletic performance
- Scholastic excellence
- Extracurricular activities
- Joining "in" groups
- Drinking alcohol or taking drugs
- Proving they have "guts" (taking risks)

Physically attractive teenage girls seek recognition by being popular with the "right" guys. Less attractive girls either role-play or offer easy sex.

As in Ron's case, he chose the last two items on the list—drinking alcohol and taking risks. These, combined with the rebelliousness that is common in the rejected, led him into the criminal life.

Dr. Carlos Garelli, a professor at the University of Buenos Aires in the department of child development has stated rejection's effect this way:

"Infancy, childhood and adolescence are seen as sensitive periods during which attachment develops, normally or deviously, according to the experience the individual has had with his attachment figures.

"Psychopathology generally, and felony in particular, are deeply rooted in histories of deserting, violent parents.

"Confirmed psychopaths (criminals, murderers, and other systemic social offenders such as delinquents) report histories of: early adverse parental attitudes and disrupted relationships—particularly in the presence of mother's threats of desertion as a means of discipline."

The rejected children feel a mixture of anger and anxiety, anger because they are threatened, anxiety because they fear the loss of the mother. They also fear that displaying the anger will precipitate the loss. In later adolescence and adulthood, they will display the anger indiscriminately: to siblings, friends, parents, anyone in authority, anyone who appears feeble, spouses, and children.

Chapters seven and eight describe Ron's rebellion, his hatred of anyone in authority, his need to prove that he could "stand up" to the cruelest of guards, and his determination to continue the path of a criminal. Perhaps he thought that because of his bargain with God, he needed to continue that lifestyle. Perhaps he felt that his worth and value was so limited that he could not rise above the childhood messages he had received to be anything more than what his parents saw him to be. Children rise to the expectation that their parents have of them. Altogether too many, like Ron, cannot see or believe that their heavenly Parent knows all about them and still considers them to be valuable, that, as their *real* Parent, He is eager to help them develop to their full potential.

O Lord, you have searched me and you know me.
You know when I sit and when I rise;
you perceive my thoughts from afar.
You discern my going out and my lying down;
you are familiar with all my ways.
Before a word is on my tongue
you know it completely, O Lord.
You hem me in—behind and before;
you have laid your hand upon me.
Such knowledge is too wonderful for me,
too lofty for me to attain
(Psalm 139:1-6).

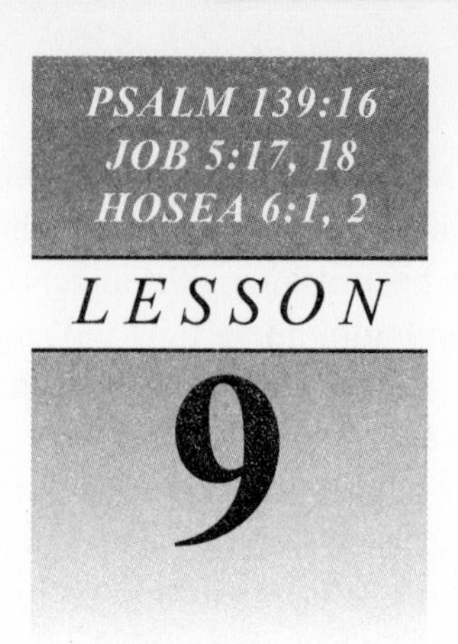

All the days ordained for me
were written in your book
before one of them came to be
(Psalm 139:16).

By this point in Ron's story, he is suffering the consequences of the choices he has made. But no, the prison torture didn't have to be a part of the consequences, you might object. Let's consider why God might have included even the barbarous attitudes and the heinous brutality of the prison guards as part of His plan. Let's consider why a loving God might have allowed Ron to suffer the humiliation of nakedness, the agony of sunburn, or the aggravation of antagonistic guards.

Just as a loving parent who sees his child heading down a steep ravine or into speeding traffic would grab his child with force and yank him back from the brink of death, so a heavenly Father would allow the pain necessary to jerk us from the tight grip of His enemy. Yes, a child snatched from danger will display the black-and-blue bruises from the tight grasp of his rescuer; he may even end up with a dislocated shoulder—but it would be a small price to pay for being saved from death. So the heavenly Father, when He sees His beloved children on a fast track to destruction, will set in their path whatever is necessary to stop them—or at least to get their attention.

The biblical book of Hosea is an allegory that illustrates the way God tries to stop His people from being hurt by the consequences of their rebellious behavior. In the story, God's prophet Hosea was instructed by God to marry an adulterous woman, Gomer, because the land was "guilty of the vilest adultery in departing from the Lord" (Hosea 1:2). Over and over again, Gomer left her husband and went out after other lovers. Each time she left, Hosea would search for her and bring her back to their home. He made every attempt to prevent his wayward wife from straying: thornbushes in her path, walls so that she could not find her way, exposure before her lovers, etc.

Hosea illustrates the role of God in the allegory. Hosea was doing for Gomer what God was doing for Ron: He was determined to persuade His son to abandon his self-destructive, rebellious behavior. He was determined to help His son find a relationship with his Father. God wanted to be to Ron far more than any earthly father could be—a model, a safe place, his security, and his hope for salvation. If that required taking His son to Shelby County Correctional Facility to be sunburned severely and to live in a cold, damp box, God would let that be. Anything to save His boy.

Blessed is the man whom God corrects;
so do not despise the discipline of the Almighty.
For he wounds, but he also binds up;
he injures, but his hands also heal
(Job 5:17, 18).

God is willing to work through even evil circumstances to entice a person to come closer to Him. The truth is that God is the One doing the enticing and using whatever means is effective to get the job done. For Ron, it took Charlie's parting words and a sign on the bulletin board. It took an antagonistic guard to egg him on, in order to get Ron to attend church a second time. God will use whatever is necessary, whatever tool He knows will do the job, and He will take whatever we can give, even if it's a sham, to attract us to Himself.

Come, let us return to the Lord.
He has torn us to pieces but he will heal us;
he has injured us but he will bind up our wounds.
After two days he will revive us;
on the third day he will restore us,
that we may live in his presence
(Hosea 6:1, 2).

PSALM 68:5, 6

LESSON 10

In the book *Letter to My Father,* Frank Kafka wrote: "I was a mere nothing to you . . . in front of you I lost my self confidence and exchanged it for an infinite sense of guilt."

Today's youth are growing increasingly distant from their fathers, largely due to the prevalence of single-parent homes in which the mother is usually the custodial parent, and to the few hours that fathers spend conversing meaningfully with or enjoying activities with their sons and daughters. Frightening numbers of boys grow up without the powerful model for manhood that they need. Many others suffer because fathers who are physically present in the home are emotionally absent from their children. The need to live like "the Joneses" has sent mothers into the work-a-day world, abandoning the nurturing role and exchanging a home-cooked meal for a TV dinner, eaten in front of the TV.

These sons marry and produce sons of their own with whom they do not know how to relate, because their own fathers did not relate significantly with them. One must possess a thing before one can give it away. One must have received from a father to be able to adequately give to a son.

This difficulty of fathers relating well with sons is not a new dilemma. Rich and poor, educated and illiterate families suffer the results of absent, emotionally distant, or abusive fathers. Winston Churchill struggled to connect with a father who either would not or could not respond. William Manchester's *The Last Lion,* a biography of one of Great Britain's powerful leaders, contains Churchill's recollection of his father:

> [My father] wouldn't listen to me or consider anything I said. There was no companionship with him possible and I tried so hard and so often. . . . He treated me as if I had been a fool; barked at me whenever I questioned him. I owe everything to my mother; to my father, nothing.

In his book *When Men Think Private Thoughts,* Gordon MacDonald states:

> What is now needed [by a growing boy] is *phallic-love.* This is a generative, energy-giving kind of love that challenges him to move ahead, to explore, to change. It motivates him to take risks, endure hardships, resist adversaries. Its energy surges outward, thrusting, creating, innovating, acquiring. In its fullest sense it is a seed-planting, generative kind of energy that is the trademark of the male nature. If womb-love (mother's love) nurtures life, phallic-love inseminates life.

MacDonald describes the man a boy needs as one who will walk alongside him, modeling, mentoring, encouraging, and challenging the boy. How many boys are fortunate enough to have a father capable and willing to do that? How many boys long simply for an acknowledgement that they are sons, and that their fathers care who they are and what they will become. In the book *Bourgeois Blues* written by *Time* magazine writer Jake Lamar, he writes:

> Try as I might to suppress the past, memories of my father came rushing back like bad dreams. Usually I'd tell myself I didn't give a [expletive deleted] about Dad or what he thought of me. Other times I felt an almost desperate need for his approval, his sponsorship in the world. Then, I'd decide I didn't want his emotional support. Just an acknowledgement. I just wanted him to recognize me, to say, Yes, you are my son, you do exist.

When Ron was in his early teens, he once asked his father why he used to beat his brother George but never touched him. The question was not, Why did he beat one son and not the other? The question was, Why didn't his dad touch him at all? His dad's response to the question was that he was trying to beat good sense into George, but since it didn't work he decided to ignore Ron to see if that would work. Obviously, Stanley's evasive answer didn't answer Ron's real question.

Here is just another example of the effect of poor role models extending over several generations. Apparently no one had taught Stanley how to connect intimately with another human. His cold, bitter mother and his distant, angry father had been his only models. He inflicted upon George the beatings he had received from his own father, and upon Ron, the distance he had felt from his own mother. As far as Ron was concerned, beating would have been preferable to the indifference. At least then he would have known that somebody cared enough to notice.

According to MacDonald, a son seeks three things from his father:

1. Common identity (his father and he are one).
2. Three assurances: he belongs, he is valued, he is competent.
3. Help to calibrate his feelings, to formulate his responses to situations, and to control his appetites and passions.

Looking back at Ron's childhood, it is clear that he received none of the three from Stanley. How could Ron ever believe that his heavenly Father wanted to lavish on him what his human father could not give him? If Ron was ever to understand a Father he couldn't see and experience physically, another person would have to stand in the gap, someone who would demonstrate the qualities that Ron had expected in his father.

There had been several who had stood in the gap before Leonard entered Ron's life: Grandpa Miller, Johnny, Charlie Ward, and W. B. Blanton. They were messengers, preludes to the one who would more completely become Ron's father figure—Leonard Haswell. They helped lay the groundwork; they showed the caring, the compassion, the concern of God to a boy whose representation of God in childhood, his human father, had himself, never had a father he could count on. All along the way, God was working to reveal Himself to His son, to connect with him in a way far superior to what any earthly father can. Carefully, through surrogates and through life circumstances, He gave the rejected son a taste of the relationship that was to come.

> A father to the fatherless, a defender of widows,
> is God in his holy dwelling.
> God sets the lonely in families,
> he leads forth the prisoners with singing
> (Psalm 68:5, 6).

Scores of Christians cannot answer basic questions about their identity. Their confusion is revealed in statements such as, "I don't know who I am," or, "I'm not sure what God wants from me or if He even cares." Why are so many people working jobs that they dislike, attending churches that leave them empty after every service, and trying to connect with people who can't connect? Why don't they know who they are?

We use religious jargon to make our answers sound good. "Why, you're the son or daughter of God!" "You are a gifted, talented individual, whom God wants to use to reach unsaved people for Him!" But in times of silent reflection, those answers do not ring true. Why?

As a society, we have become increasingly disconnected from intimate relationship with fellow human beings. We continue to long for intimacy, but it eludes us. If we were truly born to have an intimate relationship with God, why can't we achieve it?

The Old Testament gives an answer to this question in Isaiah 59:2. "Your iniquities have separated you from your God; your sins have hidden his face from you, so that he will not hear."

"What have I done that's so offensive to God?" we ask. "I haven't killed anyone or committed adultery. I do my best to honor my parents." Part of the answer is that that Jesus took the commandments of stone and converted them into flesh. He transferred the Decalogue from external behavior into the mind, into the thinking and the intent of the heart. But before you feel even more guilt, let's explain a bit more exactly what we mean.

Satan's agenda is to damage us during our character-forming years so that we will grow up to be warped and wounded adults who will pass on this affliction to subsequent generations—to our own children. The damage we received by not getting our basic emotional needs met or by being abused by rejection, sexual exploitation, or emotional or physical cruelty creates within us a need to satisfy our own emptiness, to fill our own emotional needs. We become self-centered. Our compulsion to satisfy our emptiness turns our focus so totally on self that there is little room for intimacy with God or others. We are shackled by our drive to satisfy needs that cannot be satisfied from the outside.

Such insatiable hunger must be satisfied from within. But when the human mind is filled with its own pain, there is no room for the Savior, the Great Physician who has the power to heal the pain. There is also no room for the presence of even a child or a spouse. We want what we want, when we want it!

Ron wanted out of prison! At first he was willing to buy freedom at any price. As the Holy Spirit worked in his heart, he began to evaluate the price that physical freedom would cost. He grappled with hard questions: Was he converted? Was he a fraud? Was disappointing Leonard too high a price to pay for freedom?

If you were a Northerner, locked in a Southern prison, what would you be willing to pay to get out? Eventually, Ron's dozens of questions were distilled into the choice between pleasing self and pleasing God.

Blessed is he whose transgressions are forgiven,
whose sins are covered.
Blessed is the man whose sin the Lord does not count against him
and in whose spirit is no deceit.
When I kept silent,
my bones wasted away
through my groaning all day long.
For day and night
your hand was heavy upon me;
my strength was sapped
as in the heat of summer.

Then I acknowledged my sin to you
and did not cover up my iniquity.
I said, "I will confess my transgressions to the Lord"—
and you forgave the guilt of my sin
(Psalm 32:1-5).

2 CORINTHIANS 6:18

LESSON 12

How do you say goodbye to a father you've just come to know? How do you find the courage to leave the familiar and step out into the vast unknown? I'd never been a Christian on the outside, and it was a bit intimidating to think of all the temptations that would assail me. I was frightened that I wouldn't have Leonard to walk along side me. Really, the only friends in my world were Leonard and the ones who wore the same clothes that I did behind Tennessee's bars. That Leonard seemed to not accept the only gift I could give him, the song dedicated to him, was hard for me to comprehend. He had been so affirming before this day. What had happened?

I now know something of the dynamics that transpire between two individuals who have built a relationship, when facing a change in the relationship caused by long-term geographic separation. Leonard had become my father; we both knew that. This day of departure was like my coming-out party, my bar mitzvah. He had nurtured me along my Christian pathway during these childhood years, and now I was stepping out on my own, leaving him behind as if I no longer needed him. I certainly did need him, but he didn't really know that, and I lacked the words to tell him. I just left him feeling proud, but deserted.

Gordon MacDonald, in *When Men Think Private Thoughts,* explains the separation dynamic between a father and son this way: "This process of release is often jagged, fraught with turbulent feelings. Perhaps it happens smoothly for some, a mere instant in time. For other fathers and sons it may take a while. Maybe the truth is that a man has to have gone through it before he knows what it means to him."

For sons, leaving the nest is a challenging beginning, and those properly prepared feel adequate to meet the task. Unfortunately, those who have not had a father to prepare them for departure often cannot leave, but stay tied to the apron strings of home. The words on a father's lips as the son leaves may applaud the passage, but in his father heart, there is a tearing, a breaking that cannot be revealed. Often during the few days or weeks prior to the leaving, the father is unusually hard on the son, criticizing and condemning the one who is breaking his heart. Perhaps it is one way of saying, "You can't survive without me!" The boy is shouting back just as loudly, "I'll prove to you that I can!"

Perhaps that is what was happening on that last day in the "big house." I had no idea that day that I was the only son Leonard had ever known, because I knew very little of his private life or his private thoughts. I knew less of his beginnings. In all the years since I left the penitentiary, and in all the conversations and letters we exchanged, he never revealed to me the secrets of his own heart. Perhaps he thought that revealing his thoughts and feelings would have been unprofessional, but I really believe that he stayed locked up because of the fear of what was happening to him that day—the fear of loss. In many ways, Leonard was like my birth father!

Nancy and I went to Tennessee's "big house" twice while Leonard was still able to visit "his boys" there every Saturday. Once we went to visit Reuben, and once to preach in that same chapel where I first identified a father, felt his love, and allowed him to point me to the heavenly Father. I look back on it often, and I know without a doubt, that I was drawn to the Father because He sent me a spiritual father who would fill the emptiness in my heart.

After Leonard, Pastor Damazo became my spiritual father, and then Nancy's dad, who became my own dad in every sense of the word. He encouraged me through the rough spots in our first few married years, through the life-threatening illnesses of our two daughters at birth, through the financial and academic difficulties of my college years, and the beginning years of ministry.

It was in our seventh year of ministry that Nancy's father died in my arms, just the way that Stanley, my birth father had. Fortunately, by this time, I had found my heavenly Father; nevertheless, that loss was more than devastating to me. Another of my dads, Pastor Damazo, came to conduct the funeral.

Dad's funeral was in July, and my graduation from graduate school was scheduled for the following January. Dad had attended my college graduation and was as proud as any father could be. But this event would be without a father to witness it. When a son accomplishes, a father is front-row-center to applaud, to proudly acclaim, "This is my son!" There is no greater longing than the approval of a father when the son is an adult.

Then the phone call came from Leonard, asking me to pick him up at Logan Airport. Leonard would be my father again; Leonard would applaud. He came shortly after a surgery, just like he had for my ordination. In Boston's Harvard Square German restaurant, we sat around a table for lunch before the graduation: Leonard, my mother who flew in from Milwaukee, Nancy's mother and grandmother from Connecticut, our daughters, Nancy, and I. Leonard prayed, asking God's blessing on our meal, and he prayed for "his son," as the tears flowed down his cheeks and ours.

As often happens, with the years the tables turn; the father becomes the child, and the child takes care of the father. In 1992, Leonard came to our home with his wheelchair for a two-week visit. Basically he was an invalid at that point, and I found myself in the father role and was honored to spend both the time and the effort.

A few weeks later, Leonard passed away while Nancy and I were away on a trip. We found out about his death only hours before the funeral. This was my father, and I needed to honor him, so we wrote a tribute, faxed it to the funeral home, and it was used as part of the service the next day.

The tribute read at Leonard's funeral would have been merely empty, hollow words if they lacked behaviors to match. A son honors his father by the life he leads. A father is honored by the words others say about the son, words that reflect on the value of the father. When we choose to honor our human fathers by our lives, we also honor our heavenly Father; we bring words of praise to His name from all who know us.

"I will be a Father to you,
and you will be my sons and daughters,
says the Lord Almighty"
(2 Corinthians 6:18).

PROVERBS 16:9
PSALM 31:15

LESSON 13

Surrender—the action of yielding one's person or giving up the possession of something into the power of another. Usually pictures of men and women with arms raised come to mind when we hear or read the word *surrender.* It's a forced situation, usually because a gun or some other weapon is threatening life, in which fighting back would be futile. One could resist quietly, internally, but would later suffer the consequences of concealed anger or resentment.

Will—used to express desire, choice, willingness, consent, or in negative constructions, refusal. One dictionary defines *will* as the ability to make a choice, to be free enough to have a choice.

The prerequisite for voluntarily surrendering one's will to another is trust. **Trust** is assured reliance on the character, ability, strength, or truth of someone or something: one in which confidence is placed.

Trust is developed in the first eighteen months of life, according to Eric Erikson, and is based on the relationship with parents and/or significant caregivers during that time. If the parents are able to meet the child's physical and emotional needs, and are present so that they can be counted on during the first months of life, then a child develops a healthy sense of trust. Inability to trust indicates that the basic physical and emotional needs were not met or that some damage came to the person in those early childhood years. Being unable to trust creates internal anxieties.

Ron's first eighteen months of life were filled with experiences that striped him of the ability to trust anyone but himself. Such an individual becomes self-centered and self-sufficient. However, the privilege of relying on himself was removed the minute Ron walked into the first prison. His escape gave him a short reprieve from being controlled, until the choices he made led the Federal Penal System to take his freedom away again. In this chapter, we find circumstances, once again, striping him of control. That lack of control for one who is used to being "in charge" is beyond threatening.

In this situation, helpless to orchestrate people, finances, and the judicial system to meet his need for release, God had Ron, once again, where He could get through and Ron would listen. Isn't it amazing that the two keys to Ron's being teachable were (1) sending the right messenger—another father figure and (2) Ron's inability to control his circumstances? There stood God before him, creating a crisis that made it necessary for Ron to surrender, to give up on having it his way, and acquiesce to God's leadership.

Full surrender to His will is what God seeks from all of us. He endeavors to teach us that being willing to be out of control and to be under God's control means that we will always be in control. Does that sound like double talk? Perhaps, but it is not!

Spend a few moments thinking about it. Ask yourself how much relief you felt when you got out of the driver's seat and let God take the wheel. Look at all the worry you can release. In Isaiah 30:15 we read: "This is what the Sovereign Lord, the Holy One of Israel, says: 'In repentance and rest is your salvation, in quietness and trust is your strength, but you would have none of it.' "

Once Ron was able to let go of His agenda and let God make the plans, the fear and tension he had felt vanished. He was then able to pray: "Since You, God, can see the end from the beginning, since You can raise the dead to life, I guess You'll be able to direct the circumstances of my life, so that the end, which I cannot see, will be a better and brighter beginning, which You can see."

In his heart a man plans his course,
but the Lord determines his steps
(Proverbs 16:9).

My times are in your hands;
deliver me from my enemies
and from those who pursue me
(Psalm 31:15).

If We Could See

If we could see what God can see
as He looks down on us,
I think that we would be surprised
how things have turned out thus.

If we could see what God can see
as He looks back in time,
we'd see that in our fear-filled times,
into His lap we'd climb.

If we could see what God can see
if we knew Satan's games,
we'd be prepared to be one up
to counteract his claims.

If we could see what God can see,
if we knew those He knows,
we'd leave the future in His hands
unconcerned about our foes.

If we could see what God can see
observing heaven's clock,
we'd find that His time's always right

He knows just when to knock.

If we could see what God can see
'round every bend and turn,
we'd choose the path that He has forged
that lesson we would learn!

Surrender to God
I cannot change my spots.
I cannot fight alone against God.
I'm powerless in this situation.
I'm tired of trying to make my life work
according to my plans!

Finally, because you've totally exhausted your resources, you say, "I give up! You can have me; all that I am and ever hope to be is Yours. All that I despise about myself and wish I could change, I give to You to change. Everything written on my agenda, You can erase; I'll take Yours!" And then you must leave the results of that choice to God. Reading again in the book *Steps to Christ* in the same chapter where Ron read the paragraph that changed his stubborn will, that made him surrender, we find:

> Let your prayer be, "Take me, O Lord, as wholly Thine. I lay all my plans at Thy feet. Use me today in Thy service. Abide with me, and let all my work be wrought in Thee." This is a daily matter. Surrender all your plans to Him, to be carried out or given up as His providence shall indicate. Thus day by day you may be giving your life into the hands of God, and thus your life will be molded more and more after the life of Christ.
>
> A life in Christ is a life of restfulness. There may be no ecstasy of feeling, but there should be an abiding, peaceful trust. Your hope is not in yourself; it is in Christ. Your weakness is united to His strength, your ignorance to His wisdom, your frailty to His enduring might. So you are not to look to yourself, not to let the mind dwell upon self, but look to Christ. Let the mind dwell upon His love, upon the beauty, the perfection, of His character (p. 70).

Our tendency is to bang our gavel on the polished court bench of heaven and like a judge, call out, "Court is in session! The honorable ME is presiding." We want to put God on trial for the way He has led us since our conversion, for the faults of others that caused us suffering, and for the life circumstances that annoy or displease us. We choose to blame Him for the garbage while gloating over our accomplishments. We conduct the trial, convict, and choose to punish, all in one brief appearance.

But God's timing is perfect. The conclusions of the Great Judge are always right, even if we protest. Neither one day sooner, nor one day later than how He has it planned will do. We are the ones who pay the price for being in contempt of the court. And He knows that some things He has planned for us are worth the wait—even behind bars!

"I know the plans I have for you,"
declares the Lord,
"plans to prosper you and not to harm you,
plans to give you hope and a future"
(Jeremiah 29:11).